D0914013

BRITISH EMPIRICISM AND
AMERICAN PRAGMATISM

BRITISH EMPIRICISM AND AMERICAN PRAGMATISM

New Directions and Neglected Arguments

by

ROBERT J. ROTH, S. J.

Fordham University Press
New York
1993

Library of Congress Cataloging-in-Publication Data

Roth, Robert J.
  British empiricism and American pragmatism : new directions
and neglected arguments / Robert J. Roth.
      p.   cm.
  Includes bibliographical references and index.
  ISBN 0–8232–1391–9. -- ISBN 0–8232–1392–7 (pbk.)
  1. Empiricism. 2. Philosophy, British. 3. Pragmatism.
4. Philosophy, American.   I. Title.
  B816.R68 1993
  144'.3'0973--dc20   93-3064
                                                                 CIP

Printed in the United States of America

CONTENTS

PREFACE

IT IS NOT UNUSUAL for philosophers to talk about the various "turns" that philosophy has taken in the course of its history. By this they mean new directions begun by individuals or traditions that have departed significantly from previous currents of thought. Thus Socrates initiated the "turn inward," away from a consideration of the material cosmos and toward the person as a citizen of the *polis*. Descartes took the "subjectivist" or "epistemological turn" toward the self as the starting point and foundation of knowledge. There followed the "empiricist turn" as a reaction against rationalism, quickly succeeded by the "Kantian" or "idealist turn." In more modern times, we have become familiar with the positivist, linguistic—may we even say deconstructionist?—turns, proceeding successively or sometimes simultaneously. It can be argued that none of these directions represented a totally new beginning, wholly detached from what went before. Socrates had roots in the pre-Socratic tradition, and Descartes was more of a medievalist than he himself realized. Moreover, the turns that were taken were not one-dimensional, focusing on a single issue, but included many problems clustered tightly or loosely around a central perspective.

I have tried in the present volume to describe the "pragmatic turn" in relation to British empiricism. Over many years of teaching and writing on British empiricism and American pragmatism, I have long been conscious of the influence of the former on the latter. This does not imply any great insight on my part, since to anyone working in these two traditions the links between them as well as their sharp differences are readily apparent. But it is only lately that I have focused more directly on some specific problems with which the pragmatists have taken issue with their predecessors and have given the empirical tradition new directions. Moreover, there is no attempt to repeat or supplant other fine works that have already been done on empiricism and pragmatism. I have simply selected a number of themes which in my opinion have not been sufficiently aired and which deserve further consideration. These can be called "neglected arguments," an obvious reference to Peirce's defense of theism, though with a different purpose.

The philosophers treated are the empiricists John Locke and David Hume and the pragmatists Charles Sanders Peirce, William James, and John Dewey. Not all five philosophers have discussed explicitly and in detail every topic included in this volume. For example, Hume and Peirce did so regarding necessary connection and causality, but not Locke and James. But it is possible to draw from the writings of the latter two their own positions on these topics.

There will indeed be some overlap between my own explorations and those of others. After all, what new can be said on the pragmatic notion of experience? But I am pretentious or deluded enough to think that I can offer some new and perhaps even controversial interpretations which may prompt others to go back and read these philosophers from a fresh perspective. In the long run and in true pragmatic fashion, I shall have to wait for the consequences as expressed by the reactions of whatever readers may peruse these pages!

ACKNOWLEDGMENTS

I wish to acknowledge with gratitude the editors of the following journals for giving me permission to use, with some modifications, articles of mine which they have published: "Hume's Theory of Human Nature and Community," *The New Scholasticism*, 57 (1983), 331–51; "Did Peirce Answer Hume on Necessary Connection?" *The Review of Metaphysics*, 38 (1985), 867–80; "Hume and James on Personal Identity," *American Catholic Philosophical Quarterly*, 64 (1990), 233–47; "John Dewey's 'Moral Law' Ethics," and "The Empiricism of Hume's Political Theory," *International Philosophical Quarterly*, 20 (1980), 127–42, and 31 (1991), 403–17.

Especially do I wish to thank my friends and colleagues at Fordham, Vincent M. Colapietro and Vincent G. Potter, S.J. They have read large portions of the manuscript and have offered wise counsel. I have not always followed their advice regarding Peirce and James. But they have undoubtedly prevented me from making many more mistakes than the ones that may be evident in my own rendition.

My thanks are due also to the following: Mrs. Lydia Ocasio, who typed the manuscript with great efficiency and extraordinary patience; Ms. Nancy McCarthy, Fordham University Director of Research, who kindly made grants available to me at critical stages; and Dr. Mary Beatrice Schulte, Executive Editor of Fordham University Press, who by her competence, graciousness, and buoyancy has seen this volume, as so many others, to completion.

ABBREVIATIONS

For complete information regarding these abbreviations, see Bibliography.

John Locke
EU   *An Essay Concerning Human Understanding*
T2   *Second Treatise of Government*

David Hume
E   *Essays Moral, Political and Literary*
EN1   *An Enquiry Concerning Human Understanding*
EN2   *An Enquiry Concerning the Principles of Morals*
H   *The History of England*, 6 vols.
T   *A Treatise of Human Nature*

Charles Sanders Peirce
CP   *Collected Papers of Charles Sanders Peirce*, 8 vols.

William James
MT   *The Meaning of Truth*
P   *Pragmatism*
PP   *The Principles of Psychology*, Vol. I
PU   *A Pluralistic Universe*
WB   *The Will to Believe and Other Essays in Popular Philosophy*

John Dewey
EW   *The Early Works of John Dewey, 1881–1898*
MW   *The Middle Works of John Dewey, 1899–1924*
LW   *The Later Works of John Dewey, 1925–1953*

1

EXPERIENCE

AT THE OUTSET, I shall make two statements which may seem conflicting. The statements are these. The key to clarifying the similarities and differences between empiricism and pragmatism is experience. But at the same time, the term "experience" is extremely broad, even ambiguous. In ordinary discourse, experience is called mental or psychological and taken to be, or to have something to do with, consciousness or awareness. Though early forms of behaviorism seemed to deny consciousness even to humans and to describe the mental purely in terms of overt behavior, consciousness was never completely excluded, and recent modifications within behaviorism itself have given more scope to what traditionally have been called conscious phenomena. During the medieval and scholastic period of philosophy, it was usual to divide consciousness into the cognitive and the affective, the former dealing with knowing, judging, reasoning, sensing, and the latter with willing, feeling, emotion, striving. In turn each division had its own subdivision into sensory and intellectual, the former being material and the latter spiritual.

Though Descartes has too easily been accorded the honorific title of "the father of modern philosophy," he did set new directions in the history of philosophy. The factors that inspired these directions and the form that they took are too diverse and complex to rehearse now and would not be relevant to our present purpose. What is significant is that Descartes turned the attention of philosophers to epistemology. For one thing, while the medievalists were more concerned about how and what we know, Descartes raised doubts about whether the mind could know at all. Moreover, in raising his doubt, method, or otherwise, he concentrated on subjective mental states and broke the connection between mind and reality. He left himself and subsequent philosophy with the problem as to how subject and object could be joined again. Finally, in defining the self as something that thinks, he stated that a thinking thing is one "which doubts, understands, affirms, denies, wills, refuses, and which also imagines and feels." Though he held the distinction between a spiritual soul and a material body, his account of thinking brings together, in an undifferentiated collection, acts of the mind which had formerly been carefully sorted into intellectual and sensible.

It is well known that, after Descartes, philosophy took two divergent paths, one empirical, the other idealist. It is the former that will engage our attention for the most part. My task will be to trace empiricism as it developed through Locke and Hume and as it influenced Peirce, James, and Dewey. The unifying element will be their account of experience. It is important to note, however, that in calling experience the unifying element, I make no claim that all five philosophers were in complete agreement as to what experience is or even that there was accord among those in each tradition. Let us say that there are enough similarities to put them into a family of philosophers but that the differences are significant. These differences can be expressed in a general way by saying that what mainly separated classical empiricists and pragmatists was the contrast between atomism and unity, diversity and identify, discontinuity and continuity. This contrast was the source of the divergent paths which they took regarding the themes to be discussed.

LOCKE

According to Frederick Copleston, Locke was the first philosopher to devote his major work to an investigation into the scope and limits of human understanding.[2] This was *An Essay Concerning Human Understanding*. Copleston adds that the *Essay* was one reason for the dominant place of the theory of knowledge in modern philosophy. In the opening paragraph of "The Epistle to the Reader," Locke with many a rhetorical flourish sings the praises of the understanding, "the most elevated faculty of the soul," and he compares the search for truth to that of hawking and hunting in which the pursuit itself is a source of delight and pleasure. A few lines later, in more prosaic fashion, he states why he had embarked on the hunt in the first place. A group of a half dozen friends were discussing a certain topic, and several difficulties arose which prevented them from coming to any resolution of the topic. It became apparent to them that it was necessary to examine the abilities of the understanding and Locke volunteered to write a short piece on the subject (EU 7).[3] What he at first thought would require only a page turned out to be a gigantic project, written over a period of many years with constant interruptions, requiring some 700 pages, and completed when he was fifty-eight years old! The purpose of the *Essay* was to delve into the origins of human knowledge, its extent and certainty, and the basis and nature of belief, opinion, and assent (EU 44).

Book I is a lengthy refutation of innate ideas. At its close, Locke states that his attempt will be to establish principles other than innate ideas by which he can achieve his goal. For their validity he will appeal to "unprejudiced *Experience*, and Observation." But it becomes clear at the very beginning of Book II that what he takes to be experience and observation is primarily a reflection on and analysis of the contents of the mind (EU 103–104). Book II can be called an inventory of ideas. Locke looks within the storehouse of the mind and attempts to sort out the various ideas that are found there. Without going into too great detail, the following divisions and subdivisions may be noted. The first are simple ideas, derived from senses (light, color, taste, smell, extension, figure) or from reflection (understanding, willing) or from a combination of both (pleasure, pain, existence, unity, power). In these ideas, the mind is mainly passive. The second division includes complex ideas, in which the mind combines, compares, and separates simple ideas. Among these are ideas of substance, material bodies, cause and effect, and personal identity. Several characteristics should be noted regarding Locke's ideas. First, they are undifferentiated; that is, they are all of the same kind, limited to sensation. The distinction between intellectual and sensory knowledge, the spiritual and the material, going back as far as Plato through the medievalists to Descartes, is abandoned. Thinking and willing, ideas of substance, are all on the same level as color, taste, and smell. It will be recalled that Descartes too gave a similar undifferentiated inventory when he defined soul or mind as a thinking, willing, sensing, imagining being. We know, however, that he did retain the spirituality of the soul and the higher status of intellectual powers, though he never adequately explained how soul could sense when its nature was so different from the body. Nor did he give a satisfactory account of the relation of soul and body in sensation.

A second characteristic of ideas for Locke is that they are mental phenomena, the immediate objects of the mind, and known by a process of reflection. Now, it would seem that his division of simple ideas into those of sense and those of reflection would indicate that not all ideas are known by reflection. But it should be remembered that this distinction is based on the *origin* of the ideas, not on the process by which they are known. Ideas of sense arise from outside objects. It is clear, however, that what he has to say about the *nature* and *characteristics* of these ideas is derived from reflection on internal experience. Much later, in Book IV, he will examine more explicitly our knowledge of reality—our own existence, God, and external objects. But the starting point has to do with ideas and their subdivisions known through internal experience. It is this second characteristic which, I believe, illustrates most clearly that, for all his opposition to innate ideas and his insistence on the importance of sensation, Locke's experience was primarily a reflection on internal mental states. This made it extremely difficult for him, as it was for Descartes and the Cartesians, to develop a coherent theory of knowledge and of reality.

Third, Locke's distinction between simple and complex ideas is particularly important for his theory of substance. This topic marks a crucial step in his empirical philosophy and set a new trend in metaphysics. During his studies at Oxford (1652–1658), he took the usual undergraduate curriculum and also qualified for the M.A. He must have been acquainted with Aristotelian logic, metaphysics, and ethics, but it was undoubtedly the desiccated Aristotelianism of the late- and post-medieval period. In a letter he claimed that he had lost a good deal of time in his studies "because the only philosophy then known at Oxford was the Peripatetic, perplexed with obscure terms and useless questions."[4] Certainly his presentation of the "Peripatetic" theory of substance which he criticized is, to say the least, naïve. Locke remained at Oxford until 1665 as Senior Student and Lecturer, and he became increasingly interested in science. He met Robert Boyle, and they remained close friends until the latter's death in 1691. Boyle was a member of the discussion group mentioned by Locke in "The Epistle to the Reader" which eventually developed into the Royal Society. It is not clear whether Boyle was present at the session, sometime in 1670–1671, which prompted Locke to begin his long study of the human understanding.[5]

In any case, Locke set out to develop a theory of substance in accord with his sensist epistemology and Boyle's corpuscular theory of matter. He deals first with the "notion of pure substance in general." He recalls that we have in the mind a number of simple ideas, from either the senses or reflection on our own operations. We are aware that some ideas constantly go together, and since we cannot fathom how they could exist themselves, we suppose some "substratum" or "substance" in which they subsist and we give them a common name. Our idea of substance in general, then, is only a supposition of some we-know-not-what support of various qualities. We talk like children who, not knowing how to answer when questioned about what a thing is, simply say that it is "something." In actuality, the idea is some unknown support of qualities which we cannot imagine to subsist without such support. Hence we use the word substance, which means simply "standing under" or "upholding" (EU 295–96).

Such is the idea of substance in general. But we also have ideas of particular sorts of substance, first material objects, such as man, horse, gold, water. These are formed by combinations of simple ideas which "by Experience and Observation of Men's Senses" we observe to exist together. Such ideas would be bright, hot, round, or the power to produce heat and cold in us, or the power of one body to produce changes in another body. The same is true regarding the simple ideas of our own mind or ideas of reflection, such as thinking, understanding, knowing, or willing. From these we form the complex idea of an immaterial spirit in which these ideas co-exist. But the idea is as obscure as our idea of corporeal substance. In both cases, it is an imagined support of ideas called "accidents" (EU 296–98, 305–306).

When one reads Locke's description of ideas, one cannot help but get the impression that through experience and observation we begin with simples. This is true when he begins the discussion of ideas in Book II of the *Essay*. Later in the book, when he takes up the question of substance, he states *first* that the mind contains a great number of the simple ideas, *then* that we notice that a number of the simples constantly go together, with the result that we form the complex idea of substance. Once the "obscure and relative" idea of substance in general is formed, we "come to have" ideas of particular kinds of substances by "collecting" these combinations of simple ideas into one complex idea. The description is the same regarding the complex idea of spirit. We "put together" the simple ideas of thinking, etc., into a notion of immaterial substance (EU 296–97).

If we press the language that Locke uses, it would not seem unreasonable to conclude that, in his view, we first experience simples, the "building blocks," and then form complexes. Of course, one could respond that there are two ways of approaching the knowing process: one is synthetic; the other, analytic. In the former view, we first grasp reality as wholes, and it is only by a later process of analysis that we describe it by breaking it down into its components. Though this is a plausible explanation of how knowing occurs, it is not clear that this is the one Locke used. The textual evidence seems to warrant the claim that for him analysis occurs first, both in experience and in his description of that experience. In other words, the simples are primary. But even if this rendition is not entirely faithful to Locke's procedure, his emphasis on simple ideas greatly influenced his own view of experience as well as that of Hume and of the whole course of British empiricism.

Our interest in Locke's theory of substance in this chapter has been concerned mainly with what it tells us about his notion of experience. But other aspects are also worthy of note. As has already been observed, he would have been exposed to Aristotle at Oxford as that tradition came down through a narrow scholasticism. Hence he rejected the husk of the notion of substance which he took to be some kind of permanent, inert substrate to which accidental qualities are attached. He was completely unaware of the richer notion of substance as a dynamic source of activity manifesting itself through its powers and potencies in both substantial and accidental ways. Moreover, it is not at all clear that Locke denied the reality of substance even in the imperfect understanding which he had of it. He does not claim that substance does not exist but only that we have no clear idea of it. Further, the *supposition* that substance exists is an *inference*, from idea to reality, which is not capable of being justified by his own empiricism. For all that, Locke was extremely influential in closing the door on the metaphysics of an abiding entity continuing through various changes and in opening the way to some form of atomism which has become a characteristic of the empiricist tradition.

HUME

In addressing Hume's theory of experience, it would save a good deal of time and effort if one could simply say that it is a continuation of Locke's position. In some respects this is true, and yet there are notable modifications. In the Introduction to *A Treatise of Human Nature*, Hume reveals a state of mind not unlike that of Locke in the beginning of the *Essay*. Both were grappling with perplexing problems, and both saw that there was need for a re-examination of the process of knowledge. But if we compare Locke's "Epistle" and Hume's Introduction, we find that the latter is more ambitious and envisions a wider scope. The *Essay* concentrates on human understanding while Hume writes a science of human nature. Such a science is the only foundation of mathematics, natural philosophy, morals, religion, and politics, and in turn the foundation for this science of human nature is *experience* and *observation*, terms used also by Locke.

The central issue is again experience. As Locke did in the *Essay*, Hume begins the *Treatise* with a reflection on the perceptions that he finds in the storehouse of the mind. "All the perceptions of the mind resolve themselves into two distinct kinds, which I shall call Impressions and Ideas" (T 1).[6] The divisions and subdivisions are as complex and as bewildering as Locke's. But while Locke had two main categories, simple and complex ideas, Hume proposes three divisions of perceptions: (1) original impressions or impressions of sensation which initially and directly affect the soul, such as cold or heat, thirst or hunger; (2) ideas which are copies or faint images of original impressions; and (3) impressions of reflection or secondary impressions deriving from our ideas, such as passions, desires, emotions, and, importantly, a sense of virtue and vice (T 1–10, 275–76). Underlying these divisions is his insistence that every idea must have a corresponding impression, either of sensation or of reflection.[7]

Some of the characteristics of the contents of the mind are similar in both Locke and Hume and they can be stated briefly. They are undifferentiated and they are mental constructs detected by reflection. A notable difference, however, is that Locke has two main divisions of ideas, namely, simple and complex. Hume puts the distinction between simple and complex in two places, the first under original impressions or impressions of sensation, and the second under idea. Examples of simple original impressions are color, taste, and smell, while an apple is an original complex sensation. Each of these has a corresponding idea. Hume is surprisingly brief on this point. He merely states that in an apple the simple impressions are "united together" in a single object. And yet they are all original impressions. It would seem, then, that both simple and complex impressions are equally "original," and that the distinction between analysis and synthesis and the problem as to which comes first does not appear, as it did for Locke. But at the same time he makes the point that qualities such as color, taste, and smell are readily perceived to be different and can be distinguished from one another (T 2). He states further that the complex, both impressions and ideas, are "formed" from the simples. Again, when one wishes to give a child the idea of a color such as scarlet or orange, or of a taste such as sweet or bitter, one presents the "objects" so as to give the child the appropriate impressions. It would seem, then, that despite Hume's category of original impressions, he exhibits the same "building block" approach to perceptions as Locke did regarding ideas. In the next section, we shall have occasion to see if Hume is thoroughly consistent on this point.

Early in the *Treatise* Hume takes up the notion of substance, and it can be looked upon as an important step in justifying his empiricist claim that epistemology has a sensist foundation (T 15ff.). For the idea of substance had long been held as a primary case of non-sensible or intellectual knowledge. In accordance, then, with his insistence on the need for an impression for every idea, he addresses those philosophers who claim that we have a clear idea of substance and accident, and he challenges them to point out the impression from which the idea of substance is derived. It cannot arise from impressions of sensation, for substance could not be a color or sound or taste; nor could it come from impressions of reflection, for these are passions and emotions. There is only one alternative left. The idea of substance must be a collection of simple ideas, united by imagination and brought together under a single name. (Hume seems to have forgotten that he allowed for an original *complex* impression of sensation!) The mind refers these particular qualities to an "unknown something" in which they are supposed to inhere.

Now, all this reads like vintage Locke, but there is a notable difference. Locke seemed willing to admit, or at least unwilling to deny, that real substance exists. He supposes, or, better, infers, the support of qualities or accidents even though our idea of it is quite vague—"I know not what support." Hume goes further. He resists calling substance even some vague support and limits the idea of it to a collection of simple ideas united under a common name. Now, it is true that we ordinarily refer these particular qualities to an unknown "something," but this "something" is a fiction (T 6). A more discerning mind recognizes it as such and observes that the particular qualities are closely and inseparably joined by the relation of contiguity and causation with the help of the imagination.

Hume develops this line of thought at greater length in a later section of the *Treatise*, entitled "Of the Ancient Philosophy" (T 219ff.). He points out what he takes to be an evident contradiction in our view of substance. On the one hand, "the most judicious philosophers" are aware that the ideas they have of bodies are but collections formed by the mind of the ideas of the qualities that compose the object. These qualities are *different, distinguishable, separable* from one another, such as color, taste, solidity. Yet the mind is prone to regard compounds as one thing, continuing the same despite considerable changes. We have then a contradiction—composition *vs.* simplicity, variation *vs.* identity. The problem is to explain the cause of these contradictions and the means by which we attempt to conceal them.

Unity and continuity are explained by the fact that, though the qualities are distinct and successive, the mind is carried along from one to another by "an easy transition" which is the effect or indeed the essence of relation. With the help of the imagination, the mind looks upon the related qualities as though they were one continuous object existing without change. The smooth progress of thought easily deceives the mind so that it attributes an identity to the succession of qualities. But Hume suggests that we change our method of observation; concentrate on and compare any two distinct phases of the succession and we will find that there are significant variations which destroy the identity. Whereas before the smooth progress of thought revealed an identity, the comparison of two distinct and successive qualities or moments breaks the continuity and reveals the diversity. Consequently it was the imagination that concealed the contradiction between the two views by feigning "something unknown and invisible" which was thought to continue under all changes. This unintelligible something has traditionally been called *substance* as a principle or union among qualities (EU 219–21).

It is interesting to note that Hume considers the unifying role of the mind to be more in accord with primary experience. It is, if you will, more "natural." It is only by further reflection that the mind becomes aware of the different and distinguishable qualities. To overcome this, the imagination feigns an unknown something called substance. Nonetheless, in the contradiction between diversity and identity, between separate, distinguishable, successive qualities and a unified, continuous object, Hume takes the former to be more justifiable philosophically. When dealing with substance, cause and effect, belief, personal identity, and the continued existence of objects, he is willing to admit that imagination and custom smooth over gaps and diversities. It is the "judicious philosopher" who can expose the fiction and render a true account of the state of affairs. And that true account reveals the atomic nature of experience. With Hume, the atomization of experience and reality is dominant. It was to be an essential element in later empiricist philosophers until the pragmatists.

PEIRCE

When one moves from British empiricism to American pragmatism, concentrating, as we are in this chapter, on experience, one finds oneself in a quite different atmosphere. There is no inventory of the mind, a sorting out and cataloguing of discrete and separable sensations and ideas as the building blocks of knowledge. Nor is there a sharp separation between mind and object as introduced into modern philosophy by Descartes and continued to some extent by Locke and Hume. Atomism gives way to continuity, diversity to unity, discreteness to interrelation, isolation to interaction. To establish this, the attempt will be made to uncover what the pragmatists have in common regarding their view of experience, the "common thread" that weaves its way through the thought of the pragmatists. There are certainly differences, some of them significant, among them. But these will take second place to the similarities that link them together and enable them to be grouped into a common philosophic family.

Of the three pragmatists, Peirce is the most difficult to understand, not only because of the complexity of his ideas and vocabulary but also because of the seemingly haphazard way in which he developed them. Familiar is Peirce's characterization of his thought as "a very snarl of twine" (CP 6.184),[8] while James called a course of his lectures "a flash of brilliant light relieved against Cimmerian darkness" (P 10).[9] In less dramatic but nonetheless apt terms, Justus Buchler has written that following Peirce's thought "is far less like strolling in green fields than like climbing a rocky slope"![10] But he encourages us, as I do, to attempt the climb with the promise that it will not go unrewarded.

But where to being the climb? One could start at several places, but there is one passage of Peirce which is worth a quick look because it is faintly reminiscent of William James and John Dewey. The text is tantalizingly brief but quite suggestive (CP 1.335–37). Peirce claims that some writers incorrectly identify experience with sense perception. He admits that very likely every element of experience at first is applied to an external object. We do indeed perceive objects, but for the most part "experience" is more particularly applied to an event which cannot accurately be perceived. A speeding train passes and emits a whistling sound. As it goes by, the note is suddenly lowered. I *perceive* the whistle as well as the lower note. But it requires a special kind of experience to acquaint us with *events* or changes of perception. The sudden lowering of the note causes a shock, a surprise which makes us alert to the change or contrast. It is this kind of awareness that is called "experience."

The same is true of vicissitude. We *perceive* a change in our circumstances, but we *experience* the vicissitude consequent upon the change. Again, "the concept of *experience* is broader than that of *perception* and includes much that is not, strictly speaking, an object of perception" (CP 1.337). I have said that this passage is brief but suggestive. If I understand Peirce correctly, he is indicating that experience is more than individual perception. It is a pervasive quality uniting the several sensory elements into a whole that gives a new dimension to the sensory data. From this viewpoint, perception may be considered to be a series of distinguishable elements while experience is a continuous flow. As we shall see, this meaning of experience is brought to fruition by James and Dewey. But Peirce manifests an awareness that continuity is an essential aspect of our mental states.

Taking quite a different tack, let us move on to two other key notions of Peirce's: namely, the "indubitables" and the "pragmatic maxim." These are chosen not only because they are quite familiar but also because they bring into focus an approach that is vastly different from that of the empiricists. In an early paper (1877) entitled "The Fixation of Belief," Peirce with Descartes in mind criticizes the attempt to fix belief by doubting experience. A feigned doubt is a "paper doubt" and does not stimulate inquiry; there is required a "real and living doubt." Nor does one begin with "ultimate and absolutely indubitable propositions." One begins where one is, with propositions that are called indubitable not because they are above the possibility of being doubted but because here and now they are not actually doubted (CP 5.376). If in the course of future experience something new is met that causes us to question our proposition, then we begin the process of inquiry which may confirm, alter, or reject the original proposition. Much later (1905) Peirce links this with his notion of "common-sensism," stating that we have original propositions which are called indubitable because we cannot "go behind" them and because they are acritical, that is, not subject to doubt unless there is some reason to do so (CP 5.440). On the epistemological level, much more could be said about the indubitables, common-sensism, and fallibilism. What is significant for our present purpose is that Peirce's starting point for his discussion about knowledge and the capacities of the mind is radically different from that of the empiricists. Contents of the mind are important, but he does not begin with them. Before attention is given to the knowing process, one takes the stand that the mind is already in contact with objects until it is proven to be otherwise. Surely minds and objects are different and separate, but the initial experience indicates the unity and continuity between them. Further, experience and reflection can focus on their separateness and diversity and may even reveal their incompatibility. But unity and continuity are primary in experience.

Peirce makes a similar point in his pragmatic maxim. It is found in a paper entitled "How to Make Our Ideas Clear." He is seeking a way to clarify the meaning of an idea. One quickly becomes aware that for Peirce an idea is not like that of Descartes or the empiricists; it is, rather, a proposition, an affirmation, or, even more, a belief. Moreover, it does not consist in a static content in the mind seeking its counterpart in some outside object. Belief describes how the object affects me and how I deal with or interact with the object if and when I come in contact with it. Thought is a relationship between subject and object, an interaction between them. It is in this context that he states the pragmatic maxim as a rule of clarifying ideas. "Consider what effects, that might conceivably have practical bearings, we conceive the object of our conception to have. Then, our conception of these effects is the whole of our conception of the object" (CP 5.402). Enough has already been written about the muddled state of the maxim in which some form of the term "conception" is used no fewer than five times in two sentences of thirty-three words. Basically it states that the idea of hard means nothing more than that an object will sensibly affect me in a certain way when I come in contact with it. In other words, when I touch a hard object it will resist pressure. The maxim is related to belief, since the latter is a *rule of action* dictating a set of procedures according to which I act in certain circumstances; in a sense it *binds* me to such an extent that I violate it at my own peril, for example, when I fail to duck if someone throws a stone at me. It is also a *habit of action* in that I become accustomed to and can expect such-and-such interactions on each contact. Thus Peirce can say that "the essence of belief is the establishment of habit" (CP 5.398). Habit is a disposition to act in a certain way, answering the question: "How would I act, or interact, if . . . ?"

There is much that could be said regarding Peirce's pragmatic maxim and the nature of belief. But in keeping with the purpose of this chapter, the following brief remarks may be stated. As already indicated, idea or thought for Peirce is not primarily a static, mental content but an interaction, a continuity, between knower and known. Further, the idea is developmental, that is, it is not fixed once for all but can grow, develop, even change in the light of future experience. Finally, Peirce is the first of the pragmatists to challenge the sharp division between knower and known, emphasized by Descartes and continued by the empiricists. A constant theme of the pragmatists is the rejection of the so-called "spectator theory" of knowledge, which views the mind and reality as standing apart from each other, or the mind as a kind of passive recipient, a blank tablet, on which knowledge is received.

Another key concept of Peirce's is synechism or continuity. Again, it is a complex concept with many aspects, but an attempt will be made to focus on those that are relevant to our present discussion. In connection with the pragmatic maxim, mention has already been made of belief, that is, the state of mind of the believer. There is another essential element which basically is that objects with certain qualities will act in regular ways. If this were not the case, if objects acted haphazardly, the mind could not confidently expect and predict regularities on the part of objects, and a rule or habit of action would never be established in the subject. In other words, objects tend to act in regular "law-like" ways and are not isolated events that happen by chance. The meaning of belief contains not only a logical component but an ontological one as well. A justification of the latter will have to wait until the next chapter on necessary connection, when the positions of Hume and Peirce will be contrasted. It is sufficient for the moment to say that Peirce has begun the move toward relations and continuities not only between mind and reality but among realities themselves. This move was furthered by James and Dewey, as we shall see.

JAMES

William James was long known as "the father of American prag-matism." The publication of *Pragmatism* (1908) firmly placed that tradition in the American philosophical mainstream. The new orientation that pragmatism gave to philosophy and the obscurity of Peirce's work built up the legend of James as the originator and leading exponent of the "new ways of thinking." But, as we know, the publication of the Peirce papers beginning in the 1930s rein-stated Peirce as the genuine prophet, and he has been recognized as such ever since. This would not have surprised or disappointed James, for he often recognized the debt he owed to Peirce. The best-known and most important of these acknowledgments is found in *Pragmatism*, Lecture Two, "What Pragmatism Means," in which James explicitly recounts the history of the pragmatic maxim and adopts it as his own starting point. It would seem, then, that this would be the place to begin a discussion of James, following as it does on a section about Peirce. Instead I would like to go back to an earlier work which, this time deservedly, earned for James the title of "the father of American psychology." It is *The Principles of Psychology*, published in 1890, though written over a period of a decade or more.

It is my contention that James wrote the *Principles* primarily from the standpoint of a psychologist. This does not completely exclude James the philosopher, since he was already interested in philosophical questions and since psychology was not completely separated from philosophy in American universities until well into our century. Moreover, it must be kept in mind that in the latter part of the nineteenth century psychology as a science was in its infancy and, perhaps even more importantly, it predated the rise of behaviorism. Within this context, the following can be said regarding James's view of his own project in the *Principles*.

James defines psychology as "the Science of Mental Life, both of its phenomena and their conditions" (PP 15).[11] It is positivistic and non-metaphysical, seeking to explain states of consciousness through verifiable laws that are clear and avoid dubious hypothe-ses (PP 182). The method of investigation is introspective obser-vation which we must rely on "*first and foremost and always*" and which means "the looking into our own minds and reporting what we there discover" (PP 185). The terms "introspection" and "introspective observation" occur again and again in his chapters on consciousness and personal identity. James was well aware that introspection had champions and debunkers, the one arguing for its infallibility, the other for its complete unreliability. He adopted a middle position and held that, though introspection is difficult and fallible, it is no more so than any other kind of observation. He is confident that patient effort will enable psychologists to eliminate past errors and to arrive at a consistent system that will establish a consensus, at least as far as that is possible (PP 192). James further reveals his approach to psychology when he praises Hume, and Locke as well, for taking the study of personal identity "out of the clouds" and for making it empirical and verifiable (PP 319).

What does he mean by this statement? If we consider the whole thrust of his treatment of consciousness and the self, he means two things: first, Hume has taken the study of self out of metaphysics, and second, he has applied the empirical and verifiable method of introspection. The second part of the statement would seem to be surprising and controversial in the light of contemporary treatments of self. But it is clear that, whenever James opposes Hume's theory, it is always on the grounds that Hume had made an incomplete and even erroneous reflection on our mental states. James professed to take a fresh look at these and to point out where Hume had gone wrong. This will become clearer as we proceed.

The focal point of the *Principles* are states of consciousness which are phenomena distinct from things outside the mind. James finds it difficult to choose a general term for these states, and he finally settles on either feeling or thoughts which designate all states of consciousness as such without reference to their particular quality or cognitive role (PP 185–86). In describing the nature of these states, he opposes the position of Hume and the so-called associationists. According to them, ideas are like dominoes that constantly change or pieces of glass in a kaleidoscope that are grouped together by some "fantastic laws" of association (PP 17). Or again, they have chopped up consciousness into bits (PP 233). Thought becomes a bundle of separate and discrete elements (PP 267).

In the famous Chapter IX of the *Principles*, called "The Stream of Thought," James presents his own introspective report regarding the nature of consciousness. In opposition to the atomic sequence of discrete particles as proposed by Hume, James claims that thought is continuous, where continuous means that there are no breaks, cracks, or divisions. Introspection does not reveal consciousness to be chopped up into bits. Not even words like "chain" or "train" aptly describe the experience as it first appears to us. The metaphor which he feels most naturally describes consciousness is a river or stream. From now on he will refer to it as "the stream of consciousness, or of subjective life." To illustrate his point, James uses an example that at first glance would appear to manifest the discrete character of consciousness, that is, silence broken by a thunderclap. This is an experience familiar to all of us. It would seem evident that there are two succeeding states of consciousness, one of silence and the other of shock. But James states that this description is due to a "superficial introspective view" which overlooks the affinity existing between the silence and the shock. Even when the thunder breaks upon us, the awareness of silence continues; otherwise the thunder would not cause a state of shock. A more faithful rendition of the conscious state would be to call it "not thunder pure, but thunder-breaking-upon-silence-and-contrasting-with-it" (PP 231–34). To use a Deweyan description of experience, the state of shock is prepared for, in a sense is constituted by, the silence preceding it. If the thunder continues, the experience could change from shock to annoyance. We think that the thunder wipes out the silence, but the feeling of the silence as just departed is included in the feeling of thunder (PP 234). Hence, even in this example, which seems to be an extreme case, James argues for continuity. It is, of course, more evident in less dramatic instances, where the rate of change is slower and more normal. James likens these to the flights and perchings of a bird where the flight is easy and fluid and the perchings momentary. But in this case too introspective observation can prove "baleful" simply because it is so difficult. It leads us to emphasize the resting places, and we commit "the great blunder" of overlooking the transitions (PP 236–38).

In my opinion, James's reflection on consciousness from the standpoint of a psychologist is a powerful challenge to the classical empirical theory of experience. In one sense, Hume and James are not far apart, since both conceded that the feeling of continuity was primary in experience. But there is a crucial difference. Hume attributed continuity to the deception of the imagination and left the impressions and ideas as inherently discrete. James, however, claimed that experience is inherently continuous, as he clearly illustrated by his example of silence followed by a thunderclap. It remains to be seen whether James's account will stand up when applied to particular problems. This will be examined in the chapter on the self.

The next aspect of James's thought to be considered is his theory of "radical empiricism." Its best-known formulation is contained in the Preface to *The Meaning of Truth* (1909), which was published in answer to difficulties raised by *Pragmatism*. The book is actually a collection of papers already published, but in the Preface he stated clearly the main points of radical empiricism. And yet this was not the first time that it was proposed. It began to develop as early as "The Sentiment of Rationality," an essay that appeared in 1879 and was published in fuller form in 1882. Radical empiricism emerged as an alternative to monistic or absolute idealism, which, he claimed, drew its inspiration from Hegel. It was the reigning philosophy of the German, British, Scottish, and American schools. In order to appreciate the sharp differences between absolute idealism and radical empiricism, it would be helpful to see how he understood the former and why the latter became his proposed alternative.

In "The Sentiment of Rationality,"[12] James stated that the task of philosophers is to attain some unified view of the universe that would be in the main more rational than a chaotic one. Put in other terms: it is the endeavor to remove the state of perplexity and achieve a feeling of peace, ease, and rest. But this satisfaction can be sought in either of two ways. One can adopt the simple substance of a Spinoza which unifies all parts of the world under some abstract classification but which ends up in an "empty barrenness" because the living facts of concrete existence are denied or ignored. The alternative is the "looseness and separateness" of Hume which attends to the individual facts but ends in an equally barren "sand-heap" world without any unifying element. As a matter of fact, James maintains, the human mind craves both unity and diversity, simplicity and complexity; and though at times it seeks comfort in a purely theoretic rationality, it is "a plaster but no cure," since the particular aspects of real life demand attention. Consequently James feels that the preference should be given to empiricism or pluralism over idealism or monism. But it is to be an empiricism of a special kind which even at an early stage of writing he calls "radical" (WB 5) and which he develops throughout his philosophic career. In a sense, "The Sentiment of Rationality" can be viewed as a forerunner of *Pragmatism*, Lecture One, "The Present Dilemma in Philosophy," in which he makes his famous distinction between two types of philosophic temperaments, the one called the "tender-minded" and the other the "tough-minded." The former temperaments are rationalistic, idealistic, monistic, religious; they seek the unity of things and emphasize wholes, universals, abstract and eternal principles. They find these in some kind of absolute all-knower. The tough-minded are empiricistic, naturalistic, pluralistic, irreligious; they emphasize parts, the concrete facts, and see no need for something or someone above and outside the facts to bind them into a unity. He proposes pragmatism as the "happy harmonizer" of these two different and even hostile viewpoints (PP 39).

In *The Meaning of Truth*, James states that radical empiricism consists of a postulate, a statement of fact, and a generalized conclusion.

> The postulate is that the only things that shall be debatable among philosophers shall be things definable in terms drawn from experience. . . . The statement of fact is that the relations between things, conjunctive as well as disjunctive, are just as much matters of direct particular experience, neither more so nor less so, than the things themselves. The generalized conclusion is that therefore the parts of experience hold together from next to next by relations that are themselves parts of experience. The directly apprehended universe needs, in short, no extraneous trans-empirical connective support, but possesses in its own right a concatenated or continuous structure [MT 138].

The postulate is standard empiricism. In effect, it states that philosophic discourse must begin and continue with material drawn from experience, and by this he means sense experience. This places his philosophy firmly in the empiricist tradition. The statement of fact and the generalized conclusion are important additions because James is staking out a position in opposition to both idealists and classical empiricists. He claims that both are guilty of cutting reality into discrete entities. In the earlier discussion, we have seen that in *The Principles of Psychology* he had protested against Hume's view of experience as a sequence of discrete perceptions. By his reflection on the shock of the thunderclap, James argued that experience is continuous as well as discontinuous. Hume had concentrated on the disjunctions and failed to recognize the conjunctions. As a result of his views on experience, James called it a flow, a stream rather than a chain. He employed a similar kind of reflection in *A Pluralistic Universe*, published in the same year as *The Meaning of Truth*. The book comprised the 1908 Hibbert Lectures at Manchester College, Oxford, where James met and criticized the British idealists in their own camp. Chapter VII, entitled "The Continuity of Experience," is a full description of his theory of experience. This time it is directed against the idealists who accept the discrete character of experience as inherited from the empiricists. In this chapter he cites contemporary psychology as confirming his position and in a footnote refers to his earlier treatment of the "stream of thought" as developed in the *Principles* (PU 126*n*3).[13] Again he insists that radical empiricism recognizes conjunctions as well as disjunctions in experience, though, as in the *Principles*, he emphasizes the former. Sensations are a flux; "concrete pulses of experience" are not inwardly simple; they interpenetrate and are related so that the difference between the relation and what are related is difficult to detect. Even the smallest feeling is colored, as it were, by an earlier part, and there is already "the rush of thought forward" into a continuous future. In every pulse of inner life immediately present to us, there is "a little past, a little future" (PU 126–29).

But it is important to note that James is not limiting discussion to connections within *experience*. He is also arguing for connections between *things*. In *The Meaning of Truth*, the statement of fact asserts that relations between things are as much a matter of direct particular experience as the things themselves. It is clear that for James real connections exist not only between conscious states but between external objects as well. The generalized conclusion states that the parts of experience are held together by relations that are themselves experienced. Though this statement refers directly to experience, it also holds for objects. For James immediately adds that "the directly apprehended universe" needs no trans-empirical connective support since the universe itself possesses its own continuous structure. *A Pluralistic Universe* makes the same point. James states that idealists rise above concrete existence and form general concepts expressed in definitions. By itself, this creates no problem. But the concepts are then used "privatively, as well as positively," that is, since they contain only independent essences, they do not include relations and consequently exclude them. In this way the possibility of connections between things is denied. James calls this "vicious intellectualism" or "vicious abstractionism" (PU 32ff., 99). But since the idealists are driven by the desire for a unified world-view, they invoke some absolute and external mind to connect things together. In sum, though commentators have given more attention to James's emphasis on connections within experience, he also insisted that there are natural connections between things.

To illustrate this point further, our treatment of James's theory of experience will conclude where it began: namely, with his adoption of Peirce's pragmatic maxim in Lecture Two of *Pragmatism*. James's use of the maxim and his application of it to epistemological problems have been analyzed and dissected many times, so there is no need for an extended tour over familiar terrain. Our purpose will be to use it briefly as another illustration of James's insistence on continuity, this time between knower and known. For James, inquiry and knowledge do not describe what goes on merely in a totally independent mind regarding a totally independent object. They indicate a process between two components intimately related in a mutual interchange. An idea or belief is essentially an active engagement between subject and object; it is a plan or habit of action, preparing one for the kinds of interactions that can be expected to take place between the two (MT 224). Further, the knowing process is more than a truth-claim describing how objects do or can interact; it does more than merely *re-present* reality. Knowledge is also creative. When a new problem arises, one can project a plan of action and then make modifications in the surrounding conditions. If the projected solution "works," the plan is true or, to use James's term, it is "made" true and holds until it is called into question in the light of future conditions. This creative aspect of knowledge was initiated by Peirce, continued by James, and developed in far greater detail by Dewey.

James's use of the pragmatic maxim and his emphasis on continuity illustrate the connections which he held to exist between the knowing subject and external reality. I will try to show further that James recognized connections between things outside the mind. This will be done in the next chapter on necessary connection. It may seem strange to use this term in relation to James, for he never discusses it as such. The *locus classicus* for necessary connection is found in Hume and in Peirce's response to Hume. But I believe it can be shown that, while James does not explicitly use the term, he at times addresses problems which ultimately raise the question regarding the kind of connections that exists among external objects.

Dewey

Of the five philosophers discussed in this book, the term "experience" is associated above all with John Dewey. The term appears in the titles of three major books. In practically every book that he wrote, there is a section on experience. This is true even of his technical logical works. *Essays in Experimental Logic*, published as early as 1903, opens with the statement that the key to understanding the essays lies in the passages regarding the temporal development of experience. *Logic: The Theory of Inquiry*, published thirty-five years later, has many references to experience. Moreover, his early and later volumes on education, *Democracy and Education* (1916) and *Experience and Education* (1938), highlight experience. In *Experience and Nature* (1929), Dewey stated that the primary test of the value of any philosophy is its theory of experience. Finally, *Art as Experience* (1934), in the view of the present writer Dewey's richest and most beautiful book, represents the fullest explanation of his philosophy of experience. In view of all that Dewey himself published on experience and of all that has been written about his theory, it would be impossible to cover all its details. A selection will be made in accordance with the purpose of the present chapter and the chapters which follow. The order of development will be: (1) Dewey's critique of classical empiricism, (2) his basic insight enabling him to overcome its defects, (3) his notion of experience, and (4) the link between his theory of experience and his own empiricism.

Reconstruction in Philosophy (1920) is often considered to be Dewey's first formal presentation of his "experimental philosophy." The opening chapters set the historical and scientific background for the reconstruction that he was proposing. I find these chapters to be lacking in any genuine understanding of and appreciation for the origins of philosophy or for the positive contributions made by the Greek and medieval philosophers. Nonetheless these chapters give one a sense of the issues which he was confronting and which he felt needed rethinking in the light of scientific developments. Dewey's hero in making possible the reconstruction of philosophy is Francis Bacon (1561–1626), whom he calls "the great forerunner of the spirit of modern life" and "the father of induction." He forged "the new tool or organon of learning." It was a "logic of discovery" through active experimentation as the means of penetrating into the secrets of nature. It looked not to the past but to the future, namely, fruits and consequences as a procedure for discovering new truths about the universe. Research was to be carried on not by the individual inquirer but by the cooperative effort of a community of scholars. For these reasons, he calls Bacon "the prophet of a pragmatic conception of knowledge" (MW 12:94–100).[14] Dewey praises the classical empiricists too for their contribution to the reconstruction. Locke's critique of innate ideas served to unsettle the "supine acquiescence" in truths taken to be self-evident. The empiricist movement initiated by Locke attacked blind custom and arbitrary authority through an examination of the origin and growth of ideas that had been wrongly associated with dubious beliefs (MW 12:127).

And yet there was something inherently wrong with British empiricism. Citing Santayana, Dewey calls its examination of the contents of the mind "a malicious psychology." It viewed these contents as separate, discrete elements and external reality as "a heap of chaotic and isolated particulars." In the process, the mind is considered to be mainly passive, except in its ability to combine atomic sensations into complex perceptions and ideas, as described by Locke and Hume (MW 12:127–28). This attack on empiricism was not new. In an earlier essay, "The Need for a Recovery of Philosophy" (1917), Dewey had accused Hume of "pulverizing 'experience' into isolated sensory qualities or simple ideas." He called this a "stubborn particularism" and the outstanding trait of orthodox empiricism (MW 10:12).

Dewey's criticism of empiricism as just described has a good deal in common with James's. The latter too would call it a faulty psychology or, better, an inadequate reflection on experience. His solution was to return to experience and to see what had been missed. Dewey's procedure is similar. But the insights which enabled him to break through these separations among the elements of experience and between experience and nature were initially drawn from biology. As he states in the *Reconstruction*, the cardinal principle of biology is that "wherever there is life there is behavior, activity." Life even at its lowest level requires the activity of the organism adapting to its environment. And the adaptation is not entirely passive, whereby the organism is merely acted on or receives. It is action or, better, interaction between organism and its surroundings in which both are changed. So important is this interaction that it is "the primary fact, the basic category," of living things (MW 12:129–30). This theme is repeated in such seemingly unlikely works as *Art as Experience* and *Logic: The Theory of Inquiry*. In the latter volume, it is developed in an important second chapter called "The Existential Matrix of Inquiry: Biological," in which Dewey maintains that inquiry is based on biological foundations. The process of life is a continual rhythm of equilibrium, disequilibrium, and a recovery of equilibrium. At times the organism is out of phase with the environment; it feels a need, tension, a sense of dissatisfaction. It then seeks to satisfy the need by active engagement with the environment, modifying it in various ways. In higher organisms, the modifications will be quite considerable. Through activity, the organism regains its equilibrium, and a state of satisfaction is achieved. In turn, the changed environment becomes a stimulus for further activities on the part of the organism, which activities again modify the environment. And so the process continues (LW 10:18–20; 12:32–34).

From the biological model of living organisms, Dewey moves to an examination of experience, which likewise is a living process. In *Experience and Nature* he claims that the empiricists gave an

2

CAUSE AND EFFECT, AND NECESSARY CONNECTION

LOCKE

IT IS WELL KNOWN that in the *Essay* Locke wrote explicitly about cause and effect in only one place (EU 324–25). What he had to say there was brief and sketchy, and he was completely silent about the problems of necessary connection as raised later by Hume. However, if other texts are consulted, it can be seen that he anticipated several aspects of Hume's treatment and that in fact his own position is remarkably similar to that of his successor. To show this, it will be necessary to pull together passages that are scattered in several different places in the *Essay*. It is especially important to understand the interrelationship of such key Lockean concepts as quality, power, and real and nominal essence.

In dealing with qualities, Locke is doing two things. In accordance with the agenda set forth at the beginning of Book II of the *Essay*, first he is attempting to describe the variety of ideas that come into the mind, and second he wants to explain how these ideas originate. It is usual for commentators on Locke to focus on his division of qualities into primary, secondary, and tertiary. But for our purpose, it is necessary to link this discussion with what he has to say about power. For this reason, the following treatment will feature powers and their divisions as the leading categories and then show their relation to qualities.

Locke maintains that our idea of power is twofold: active, or the power to make changes; and passive, or the ability to undergo changes. The former, grasped by reflection of the mind upon itself, refers to the actions of the mind in perception or thinking, called understanding, and in volition or willing, called will. Actions of the understanding are operations of the mind about its ideas in remembering, discerning, judging, comparing, enlarging, and abstracting. Actions of the will consist in the moving of the various parts of the body (EU 127–31). Locke feels that our idea of active power in ourselves is quite clear (EU 235).

Our constant contact with external sensible objects furnishes us with the idea of passive power. But such contact gives us fewer examples of active power and furnishes nowhere near the evidence of such power as given in reflection of the mind on its own activities. The example he uses is motion. We observe a billiard ball in motion under the impact of a billiard stick (EU 235). The motion we observe is rather a passion than an action. Likewise, if the ball strikes another and puts it in motion, it only communicates to the second ball the motion it received and thereby loses as much motive force as it communicates. Locke calls this "a very imperfect obscure Idea of active Power," for by sensation we do not observe the initiation of action but only its reception. Several points can be noted here. First, Locke does not rule out the idea of active power in this example; he calls it "a very imperfect obscure idea." Further, the example of motion is a very limited one in view of the great variety of actions that are observed, some of which he himself alludes to in other places. One could ask if the limitation that he puts on our idea of active power applies only to motion, especially in view of other examples which he uses and where he speaks in terms of alterations produced by one object on another. My own reading of Locke leads me to suspect that he is more generous in his attribution of active power to other kinds of actions of sensible bodies.

It is in his discussion of simple ideas that Locke links power and qualities. In a long chapter, he sets out to explain more fully the nature of our ideas (EU 132ff.). He distinguishes the ideas or perceptions in our mind from the alterations of the matter in bodies that cause (Locke's word) these perceptions. The ideas are what the mind perceives in itself, while the qualities in the objects which *produce* (again Locke's word) the ideas are called *powers*. For example, I perceive a snowball as white, cold, and round. These latter Locke calls ideas in the mind, while the abilities in the object to produce them he calls powers (EU 134). Once this link or, better, identification of qualities and powers is made, one must always read power wherever Locke uses quality and vice versa. This is especially true when he makes his famous list of primary, secondary, and tertiary qualities under the heading of power.

Primary powers are those completely inseparable from the solid parts of bodies. Such powers produce in us the ideas of solidity, extension, figure, motion or rest, and number (EU 132, 135, 141). These primary powers or qualities, perceived especially by sight and touch, are really in the bodies as perceived, even when they are not actually sensed (EU 140). Secondary powers are capable of producing in us sensations such as colors, sounds, and tastes, and they operate by reason of their primary powers. They exist only as powers and not as perceived in the mind, though they are usually thought to exist as such (EU 137). Finally there are tertiary powers in bodies to change the bulk, figure, texture, motion of other bodies, and in turn they alter the ideas in the mind. For example, the heat of the sun can change the color or consistency of wax or clay (EU 135, 140–41).

From these distinctions it can be seen that primary powers, as their name indicates, are the most basic ones. They are primary qualities which are in bodies just as they are perceived. They are also the source of secondary and tertiary powers. Moreover, primary powers have a direct connection with Locke's distinction between real and nominal essence. It should be observed that his essence is quite different from that of the Greek and medieval notion. He is not looking for the classical metaphysical principles of material things such as form and matter. Under the influence of Robert Boyle, he is concerned with the "corpuscularian hypothesis," that is, with the unobservable and unknown minute physical particles that constitute bodies (EU 547).[1]

The question now is: Can we ever know real essences, that is, the insensible particles upon which powers depend? At one point, Locke engages in some fantasies about how different the world would appear to us if God had endowed us with sense organs many times more acute than they are now. If our hearing were increased a thousand times, the noise would be intolerable. If our vision were a thousand times more sensitive, we would come closer to detecting "the Texture and Motion of the minute Parts of corporeal things" (EU 301–304). Later he takes up the question at greater length. The discussion becomes a bit disorganized and not a little repetitive, but the following are the main points. There is an order of dependence from powers down to the insensible parts or minute particles of bodies. The secondary and tertiary powers depend on the primary, while the latter in turn depend on the insensible parts or "corpuscles." Unfortunately our knowledge of the insensible parts is very limited. Some bodies are too remote, such as the sun and planets. More to the point, the particles of bodies available to our senses are too minute to be perceived, and this keeps us in "incurable ignorance." But even if we could discern the size, shape, and motions of these particles, the mind could never discern any necessary connection between these parts and the primary qualities, or among the various primary qualities, or among the secondary qualities. The basic reason is that our knowledge is dependent on sense experience. It is true that some primary qualities have a necessary dependence on and visible connection with others, for example, figure and extension, and motion and solidity. But these cases are few. Thus one could know by experience that gold is yellow, malleable, fusible, fixed, and of a given weight. But since none of these has any evident connection with the others, we could not know that, if we sensed any four, the fifth would certainly be present (EU 546). As a result, we may have distinct ideas of the various sorts of bodies as derived from our senses, and these are sufficient "for common use and discourse." But "scientifical" knowledge, that is, certain knowledge, fails us (EU 556–57).

With this as background, let us examine what Locke has to say about cause and effect, with attention to the action of one body on another. The classic text in the *Essay* is II, xxvi, 1–3, entitled "Of Cause and Effect, and Other Relations." He states that we constantly observe that the action of heat on wax changes it from a solid to a liquid state, and that fire turns wood into ashes. We call the first a cause and the second an effect. In this text he makes no comment on whether or not there is a necessary connection between cause and effect, or whether or not on another occasion like results will follow. From this text alone, therefore, no determination can be made regarding his view of necessary connection. But from what he says about powers, it is a fair assumption that he would exclude necessary connection. The basic reason is that we do not know real essence, that is, the minute particles of bodies. Further, we cannot discern any necessary connection between the particles and their powers, or between and among the powers themselves. Given these conditions, the following would seem to follow. We cannot be certain that a body that on one occasion produced a given effect through one of its powers will produce the same effect on another occasion. In another passage, he seems to take up quite explicitly the problem of necessary connection. He states that we do not know the figure, size, texture, and motion of the ultimate parts of bodies. Consequently we do not know for certain that rhubarb will purge, hemlock will kill, or opium will induce sleep. A few instances may show that such bodies produce the indicated results, but we cannot be certain that they will do so at another time (EU 556).

There is one more point to be considered. Did Locke in fact or in principle hold that we cannot know the insensible parts and consequently the powers of bodies? If only in fact, it would mean that our lack of knowledge is due to the weakness of our senses. If these could be made more acute, then our knowledge of these would be within the realm of possibility. We have seen that Locke did refer to the inherent limitations of our senses. He was also aware of the power of microscopes. But he frequently expressed his pessimism about our ability to reach down to the ultimate constituents of minute physical particles. In effect, though he did not deny the theoretical possibility of knowing real essence, he held it to be highly unlikely. As we shall see, Hume went further. He maintained that the presence of power existing in bodies was unknowable *in principle*. His consistent theme was that, regarding matters of fact, "the opposite is not impossible" since there are no logical connections among powers in bodies.

HUME AND PEIRCE

This section will deal with both Peirce and Hume. The reason is that both philosophers raised the same kind of question. Moreover, it is clear that Peirce had Hume specifically in mind when on many occasions he attacked nominalism and defended real connections. But they differed in that Peirce defended his position from a broader perspective, enabling him to arrive at a more satisfactory conclusion. To establish this thesis, it will be necessary to focus on several aspects of their thought that bear upon the topic under discussion.

Let me begin with Hume. As is well known, he was seeking the original impression of necessary connection. He lists several other terms which are synonyms, or "nearly synonyms," for necessary connection. These are necessity, power, secret power, force, efficacy, agency, energy, cause, causation, principle, connecting principle, and productive principle (T 74, 90–91, 157, 164–65, 169). The term most frequently used, after necessity or necessary connection, is power. For the most part Hume speaks of cause and effect in the usual meaning of the term. One object produces a change in another. Thus fire warms, ice cools, food nourishes, a moving billiard ball striking another puts it in motion (T 87; EN1 33–34).[2] But occasionally he has in mind a wider meaning that includes any regular sequence of events which he calls "the laws of nature and all the operations of bodies," such as the sun rises every day or a stone when let go falls to the ground (EN1 25–26; T 124, 157). This second meaning enters more consciously into later "Humean" discussions of necessary connection. On a more technical level, it embraces the changes that occur in the natural sciences. But all these examples would be called matters of fact by Hume. Power is that in an object which enables these changes to occur.

Now, Hume uses the term power in two senses. The first designates an efficacy in particular bodies at particular times. He is willing to admit that such power exists. Past experience gives "*direct* and certain information" only of these precise objects acting only at those precise moments. Bread in the past nourished me, or, better, a body with such-and-such sensible qualities had, at that time, such power. The same can be said of all varieties of production (EN1 33–34). But this is not what Hume is after. He is concerned about power which includes necessary connection between cause and effect. This is the "true manner" of conceiving power (T 161). In the case of bread that nourishes me at a particular time, sense experience gives me information about its particular qualities—the color, weight, consistency. But this does not mean that other samples of bread must nourish me at other times or that similar sensible qualities must always be accompanied by the same powers (EN1 34). On the widest level, genuine powers would be forces or principles constantly present and operative in the many shifts and changes that occur in an uninterrupted succession in the universe (EN1 63). It is these powers that we cannot grasp. Consequently we cannot discover the ultimate connection between things. Though we suppose that they will be connected in the future, we cannot penetrate into the reason for the connection (T 91, 93). This is because our experience of sense qualities and powers shares the condition of all perceptions. They are distinct, distinguishable and separable by thought and imagination. They may be conceived as separately existent and may exist separately without any contradiction or absurdity (T 634, 636). Even if we could know powers, we would not be able to discern any necessary connection between them and their corresponding sense qualities. Given like sense qualities on another occasion or in another object, it is not impossible that different results will follow simply because the presence of these qualities does not entail the presence of powers that were active in the past.

From this analysis, necessary connection can be viewed from two points of view. One is that which usually comes to mind when one thinks of Hume's theory of causality. It is the necessary connection between cause/event and its corresponding effect/event. But more basically the problem involves the relation between external sense qualities and powers. These two perspectives are, of course, closely related. We cannot be certain about the causal sequence because we are uncertain about the relation between qualities and powers. For Hume, certainty or genuine knowledge is achieved by logical implication or the apprehension of the relation between ideas (T 166).[3] Since such a relation does not exist between qualities and powers in the real order, we cannot know or predict that powers accompanying qualities on one occasion will be present and active on another occasion. Now, it is true, admits Hume, that "in common discourse" we often affirm without hesitation that arguments from causation go beyond probability and yield a higher kind of evidence. It would be ridiculous to hold only probability regarding statements that the sun will rise tomorrow or that all humans must die, even though our assurance of these is based merely on experience (T 124). In a letter to John Stewart, Professor of Natural Philosophy, Edinburgh, in 1754, Hume maintained that he would never deny the truth or even certainty of such statements as that Caesar existed or that there is such an island as Sicily, even though they lack demonstrative or intuitive proof.[4]

Of course, none of these statements relieves the commentator of the task of interpreting precisely what Hume meant. They can be read as applying to states of mind such as belief or to the condition of objects outside the mind. They could apply to Hume as agent or Hume as philosopher. It seems more consistent with Hume's theory of belief that these remarks describe states of mind of an agent who faces the normal routine of daily life. This is more clearly the case when he admits that "none but a fool or madman will ever pretend to dispute the authority of experience" when it induces us to expect similar effects from similar objects. As an agent, he is quite satisfied that effects will not change when the sensible qualities of objects remain the same. So strong is this conviction that it will not be overturned by abstract reasoning (EN1 36–41). All this is the result of custom, the great guide to life. It is custom which enables us to expect that the train of events will follow as they have in the past. Without it, we would be ignorant of all matters of fact except those immediately present to sense and memory. We would not know how to apply means to ends in achieving desired effects. As a result, all action and in large measure even speculation would cease (EN1 44–45). Hume expresses relief that nature has not left such matters to our choice for they are too important to be trusted to our uncertain reasonings and speculations (T 187). Nonetheless he adds that no argument of philosophy can maintain the veracity of these affirmations. The philosopher "who has some share of curiosity, I will not say skepticism," seeks the foundation of these inferences. He asks on what logic, or what process of argument, these affirmations rest (EN1 36–38). The opposite of all statements regarding matters of fact is still logically possible, and no argument of reason can ever assure us that the opposite will not occur. Hume is rescued from the probability of chance by his psychology of belief.

But logic plays a commanding role as to what the philosopher considers to be reasonable, and it rules out certainty regarding matters of fact. Moreover, he places the convictions that we have as agents outside of his logic and his philosophy, and even outside of his theory of reality. Lastly, if necessary connection cannot be held to be present in the causal sequence, then predictions in the literal sense are not justified. Consequently his logic also dictates what his scientific theory will look like (T 156).

*   *   *   *   *   *

Peirce spent much of his philosophical career in attacking nominalism. He claimed that his target was nominalism of the "extremist" kind as propounded by Hume, "to whose whole method and style of philosophizing I have always been perhaps too intensely averse." In this regard, Peirce makes a very significant statement: "Moreover, instead of being a purely negative critic, like Hume, seeking to annul a fundamental conception generally admitted, I am a positive critic, pleading for the admission to a place in our scheme of the universe for an idea generally rejected" (CP 6.605). This statement is significant for a number of reasons. First, he was aware that, in sharing Hume's opposition to the claim of absolute certainty regarding matters of fact, he was aligned with Hume in being called a skeptic by "apriorians." Hence he termed himself a critic but of a positive kind because he argued for that which Hume rejected: namely, law as reality. In addition, the position he defended had to be seen as having a place "in our scheme of the universe" and not as an isolated response to an isolated problem. The meaning of these statements will become clear in the course of the following discussion.

It is important to understand precisely what Peirce was defending against Hume's attack. It was the existence of real powers in objects. On the first level, Peirce clearly affirmed what Hume admitted perhaps only for the sake of argument, that is, the existence of a real power in an object at the time that the object is active. Fire heats, ice cools, a stone falls, the sun rises and sets on a given occasion.[5] But like Hume, Peirce probed further and asked whether we can know that the same or similar object will produce a like effect on another occasion. Are there in objects real powers enabling the objects to act in the same way, and can we know that they are present and make predictions about future events? Peirce's answer is yes to all parts of the question. Powers are real and not figments of the imagination, they can be known to be present in objects, and on the basis of this knowledge we can make predictions. At this point it will be helpful to describe more fully these powers as conceived by Peirce and then to move on to an even more crucial issue which is his justification for the claim that they are real. This consideration will also illuminate his meaning of knowledge.

What, then, is a power? It is the capacity of an object to do certain things under certain conditions—to warm, to cool, to fall. An object is hard or soft "whether anyone is actually perceiving the object or not" (CP 5.430) simply because the power or capacity to produce certain effects is present even when no one is there to be affected by the object. If the object is placed in an appropriate situation, it will produce its customary effect. I can predict that a stone released will fall. Power for Peirce is a real potentiality, an actual entity, according to which an object not only produces an effect on a particular occasion, but will produce that effect in a like situation. As Vincent Potter has pointed out, a quality such as hardness or color produces its effect only when the object possessing that quality interacts with another object. Before the contact, the first object really has that quality potentially "as a real power and not just as a logical possibility." When the two objects are brought together, one can predict that the potentiality will be actualized and that the effect will follow.[6] From this description of Peirce's position on power, it can be seen how sharply he opposes Hume. For he affirms real powers in objects that operate on particular occasions and that will surely operate in the future if certain conditions are fulfilled (CP 5.425). And because these powers are real, he is also affirming necessary connections not merely between ideas but between sequences of happenings in reality.

But now we come to the crux of the matter. Hume could simply reply that it is all well and good to describe what one means by powers and to assert that they exist in reality. As a matter of fact we do make such claims. But can we give reasons to justify these claims? Hume denied that possibility while Peirce affirmed it. In examining Peirce's response, it is important to bear in mind a statement already cited: namely, that his answer to Hume must be seen against "our scheme of the universe" and not against Hume's specific and narrow formulation of the problem. To begin with, Peirce does not attempt to refute Hume's contention that, since qualities do not imply powers, the latter cannot be known. Peirce would readily grant this, if knowledge about matters of fact had to be implicative after a logical or mathematical model. Hume wins his case by definition. Instead Peirce takes a broader view and asks: What theory of causal connection makes sense, is *reasonable*, in the context of the whole scheme of things? What can we intelligently understand and reasonably affirm about matters of fact, given the present state of the universe? In place of knowledge by implication, Peirce proposes a logical principle of his own. It states that one should not block the road to inquiry by declaring a phenomenon inexplicable, but one should adopt that hypothesis which seems more faithful to the things to be explained. To suppose that a phenomenon is inexplicable is not only to fail to explain it but, more than that, to put up a barrier in the way of science and rule out of court any attempt to understand the phenomenon (CP 6.171). Integral to Peirce's principle is the assumption that the world is knowable. But the facts can be understood only through generalizations made according to the dictates of experience (CP 6.173).

Peirce's principle, moreover, is worlds apart from Hume's implicative principle. For Peirce's principle is at the heart of the scientific enterprise, while Hume's runs counter to it. Peirce states that the possibility and progress of science depend on our finding rationality, generality, or law operating in nature. Hence, science has always been, and must continue to be, realistic, that is to say, it must hold that future events tend to conform to a general rule (CP 1.20, 353; 7.186). One main reason why science assumes this principle is that it works. Science carries on its experiments and makes predictions, secure in the expectation that in the main the predictions will be fulfilled (CP 1.26). It makes more sense to conclude that real power is operative in nature. Otherwise we would be maintaining, for example, that laws are fictions, predictions are illusions, things are governed by chance and not law, and that there is no coherent theory to explain why in fact things in the universe operate with such uniformity (CP 5.101). The universe would not really be understood or rendered intelligible in any meaningful way. Hume admitted that, of all the paradoxes advanced in the *Treatise*, his theory of necessary connection was the most violent because of our strong bias riveting the mind on the contrary opinion. But he still affirmed that he had given the only reasonable account of necessity (T 167). But for Peirce there are two choices before us. One is to accept the validity of predictions based on the reality of powers in nature. The other is to call them into question and to accept a chance universe. No doubt he would also chide Hume for his effort to construct a psychological theory of belief based on propensions, determinations, pretensions, and fictions, shored up finally by custom and the need to act in daily life. Peirce would consider his own option to be more sane and reasonable.[7]

Manley Thompson claimed that Peirce attempted to prove experimentally that general principles are operative in nature.[8] In a 1903 Harvard lecture, Peirce held up a stone and predicted that it would fall if released (CP 5.93–95, 101). The uniformity with which stones fall is due either to chance or to some active principle. Since the stone does in fact fall, the second hypothesis is verified. Thompson argues that this experiment may be effective as "a kind of rhetorical maneuver directed against nominalists" whom Peirce hoped to shock into a realization of the absurdity of their position. But, Thompson contends, as a device for meeting "head on" and refuting Hume by proving experimentally that the concept of cause is justified by something in reality, the experiment begs the question. "The experiment disconfirms the chance hypothesis only to the extent that a successful prediction provides evidence of a connection not due to chance, and yet that such evidence can be obtained in this manner is just the point at issue."[9] In other words, the general principle that continued regularities give evidence of real connections is the very principle that Peirce wishes to prove experimentally, and he fails by an *ignoratio elenchi*.

Thompson's criticism is persuasive *provided* he has correctly interpreted Peirce's intention. In Thompson's view, it was to prove *experimentally* the existence of real causal principles in nature. But this does not seem to be Peirce's intention at all. Thompson's opinion is based on the second sentence of Peirce's lecture: "Suppose we attack the question experimentally" (CP 5.93). But there is much more in Peirce's whole approach which indicates that he did not mean this literally. He knew his Hume too well not to be unaware that Hume himself had shown that all inferences from experience to secret powers beg the question, for such inferences "suppose, as their foundation, that the future will resemble the past and that similar powers will be conjoined with similar sensible qualities" (EN1 37; T 91). Moreover, in his lecture Peirce acknowledges that his audience will consider it "a very silly experiment." But, he asks, how we can *know* that the stone will fall? He answers by stating what everyone in the audience will admit: we know because we are convinced by experience that objects of this kind always do fall (CP 5.96). Peirce concludes that "every sane man" will adopt this hypothesis. If anyone still doubts that the stone will fall, there are countless other similar inductive predictions that are verified all the time. The doubter will have to suppose that all of these are due to chance in order to avoid the conclusion that general principles really operate in nature (CP 5.101).

This analysis brings out several important aspects of Peirce's thought. First, his statement that "every sane man" will adopt the hypothesis seems to denigrate the nominalists who do not adopt it. If such is the case, Peirce's strong language can serve as an example of his own admission that he had perhaps too intensely opposed Hume and his nominalism. But he is more to the point when he indicates that the hypothesis of real general principles is on balance more reasonable than the hypothesis of chance. One can call this a "rhetorical maneuver" if one wishes, though I am convinced it is much more than that. But it is clearly a mistake to argue that Peirce unwittingly committed so obvious a blunder as to beg the question.

Furthermore, in the very process of defending the reasonableness of the realist hypothesis, Peirce was challenging Hume's contention that logical implication exhausts what we mean by knowing. R. Harré and E. H. Madden call this "logicism," which means that the task of philosophers is to reveal the logical form of those kinds of statements that engage their interest. They attempt to distinguish and characterize propositions in terms of their logical form. In short, rationality is limited to the canons of formal logic.[10] Accordingly, matters of fact are not knowledge, and statements about them are not rational, because they do not meet the test of formal logic. And yet in daily life we do have convictions about them and we act upon them with full confidence. In order to make room for these convictions, Hume introduced his distinction between philosopher and agent. But for Peirce there is a genuine sense in which we can say that we *know* matters of fact without demanding that such knowledge have the rigor of logical or mathematical statements. This means that judgments regarding matters of fact are not philosophically suspect, requiring some psychological apparatus to make them respectable. They can be affirmed with the reasonable assurance that they conform to reality. The affirmations are reasonable, not because they conform to formal logic, but because they make sense, or at least better sense than their alternatives. At the risk of indulging in semantics, one could explore more carefully the uses that Hume and Peirce made of the terms "reason" and "reasonable." T. E. Jessop points out that Hume uses the term "reason" in two senses. At times it means the comprehension of relationships between ideas, that is, of the logical relations of contents not claimed to be existents. This kind of reason cannot operate in the knowledge of matters of fact. On other occasions, reason is used in "a shockingly loose sense" to mean a process of the imagination of associatively determined causal inference.[11] But I would suggest that Hume slips into still another meaning, perhaps inadvertently, when he says that his position is "the only reasonable account we can give of necessity" (T 167). "Reasonable" here does not seem to mean that which is in accord with logical relations or imaginative associations but that which in the long run makes sense. But whether or not this is what Hume intended, it is certainly what Peirce had in mind when he spoke of reason or the reasonable as applied to his justification for affirming real powers or general principles.

Peirce would also claim that these affirmations are assured affirmations. They go beyond the realm of chance happenings and are in accord with scientific procedure. At the same time, in denying absolute certainty regarding matters of fact, Peirce is in agreement with Hume. In fact, he had an advantage not open to Hume in being able to draw upon the theory of evolution, which gives evidence of a changing universe. In this respect, Peirce's position was more timely than Hume's since, scientifically trained himself, he was living during the rise of evolution and scientific determinism. Hence his refutation of nominalism and necessitarianism was an attempt to bring philosophical reflection to bear upon contemporary scientific thinking.[12]

Did Peirce, then, answer Hume on necessary connection? The answer has to be no if it is posed in terms of formal logical connections between qualities and powers, between causes and effects, or between sequences of events in nature. But if the question is taken from a wider perspective, the answer in my opinion is yes. For Peirce challenged Hume's meaning of knowledge and the reasonable, as well as his selection of criteria that count as evidence for an authorized affirmation regarding matters of fact. Peirce found this approach to be more sane, more reasonable, and more in accord with "our scheme of the universe."

Before we leave Peirce, it would be well to restate the problem he faced in opposition to Hume. This will help us to identify the issues at stake in James's position on necessary connection. It is the contemporary debate between realism and nominalism. This has a long and complex history, but it can be stated briefly in terms of our present purpose. The previous discussion on necessary connection and Peirce's critique of Hume focused mainly on the former's defense of real powers in nature. But in effect he was also defending realism against nominalism. For the nominalist, generality or law is merely a convenient way of understanding individual facts, which are the only things held to be real (CP 4.1). The mind cannot know whether individual instances that occur and that are experienced will recur in the future. These instances are simple, brute unconnected facts which Peirce called Secondness (CP 1.24). The future is indeterminate and indeterminable, and one cannot know or predict the course of events in the future. In opposition to this, Peirce's realism maintained that the universal is that to which knowledge aims, and it is the most important element of being, the "real" in the genuine sense of the word (CP 4.1). Realism holds that "the being" of law will direct subsequent facts and will continue to do so in "an endless future" (CP 1.23, 536). A particular event does not merely represent something that happens here and now or that happened in the past; it also indicates what *will* happen in the future if the same conditions obtain (CP 5.425). The link between power and realism is evident. Peirce is arguing not only that objects have the power here and now to act in certain ways, but also that they have the potency to act in the same way in like circumstances at a future time according to law and that they will do so, given those conditions. In this sense, power and law are not quite the same. A power by itself expresses what an object does in fact do; law indicates what it *will* do in the future—for example, that a diamond, when drawn across a pane of glass, will scratch the surface, or that a stone, when released, will fall. From all this it follows that, for Peirce, the existent is not the same as the real (CP 5.503). The former refers to individual brute facts, while law governs facts in the future. Law, moreover, is objective and not a convenient way of joining individual instances in the mind under a common name or concept. Knowledge of the real consists essentially in grasping the general law according to which individual facts take place.

One more point should be made. It has to do with the relation between belief and realism. Peirce's theory of belief has already been treated in the preceding chapter. In terms of the present discussion, belief presupposes realism or the operation of law in the world. For a rule or habit of action is developed precisely because the believer is convinced that objects operate in regular lawlike ways. And the reason for this conviction is that science has always been and must continue to be realistic, for its very possibility and continued progress depend on it. Moreover, without real power operating according to a law, there would be no coherent explanation as to why things operate with such uniformity. This is what Peirce seems to have had in mind when he stated that "pragmaticism could hardly have entered a head that was not already convinced that there are real generals" (CP 5.503). It can be seen, then, that for Peirce power, necessary connection, realism, and pragmaticism itself are all of a piece.

JAMES

With this as background, the inclusion of James in this chapter would not seem to make sense for he said nothing about power, causality, or necessary connection. But his pragmatism had important implications for realism and nominalism, and it is in this context that his pragmatism is to be examined. Yet it would seem that any attempt to relate Jamesian pragmatism to realism is doomed to failure from the start. He is frequently portrayed as an individualist, subjectivist, particularist, and nominalist. Some criticisms of James have been quite caustic. W. B. Gallie claims that James was heir to the individualism of Western thought stemming from the Reformation; he was interested in the experience of individuals and "from the depths of his own Protestant and American soul" he was suspicious of anything that claimed to go beyond the individual.[13] Thomas Knight is a less strident though still vigorous critic. He distinguishes between realism and nominalism and identifies the issues in his assessment of Peirce and James. Peirce in "The Fixation of Belief" stated that truth consists not in any actual satisfaction but in that which would ultimately be achieved if inquiry was continued to its final limits. On the other hand, claims Knight, other pragmatists, including James, held that the satisfaction is that of the individual. "Truth is thus subjective . . . the satisfaction of one person." It was for this reason that Peirce dissociated himself from Schiller, Papini, and other contemporary pragmatists and adopted the new name pragmaticism.[14]

For all that, the bias against James regarding realism and nominalism is not without some foundation. His writings seem highly personalistic, especially those on religion and religious experience. His "Will to Believe" argument for God is often read in subjectivistic terms despite his own later regret that he did not call it "the right to believe." In logic he argued for the consideration of experience; in epistemology he put great weight on concrete, particular instances. Though later critics are perhaps more gentle, there still is abroad the opinion that, if one had to choose, James would most probably be classed more as a nominalist than a realist. In this section I shall enter the lists and "break a lance" in defense of James by trying to show that, while he did not explicitly take up the question of necessary connection or the realist–nominalist debate, he can be placed more on the side of realist than has heretofore been acknowledged. Even this modest claim may prove to be too formidable a challenge, and thus a gallant effort may be wasted. But in justice to James it ought to be attempted.

A beginning can be made by recalling what was said in the last chapter regarding James's polemics against idealism. He was trying to present a unified view of the universe that would mediate, for example, between the simple substance of a Spinoza and the "sand-heap world" of a Hume. We have seen the implications of this attempt for a theory of experience as he developed it in such works as "The Sentiment of Rationality" and *A Pluralistic Universe*. This polemic appears also in *Pragmatism*. He claimed for the pragmatist the "empiricist attitude" but of a more radical and less objectionable kind. It rejects the procedure of the "professional philosophers" (read here idealists), that is, inadequate abstractions, bad *a priori* reasons, fixed principles, closed systems, and absolutes and origins built on pretense (P 31). This theme is echoed in *The Meaning of Truth*. At one point he gives the reasons for the pragmatist view of things; it is due in large measure to the breakdown of the notion of scientific truth over the previous half-century. At that time, it was thought that the laws of nature in science exactly expressed the workings of natural events. Now scientific laws are conceded to be a kind of "conceptual shorthand," reflecting approximation rather than literal exactness (MT 206–207). As a result, pragmatism opens the way for concreteness and adequate explanations, facts and actions. He claims that as a method it is at home with all varieties of philosophy—nominalism, utilitarianism, and positivism. It espouses no particular results "at the outset, at least," or "so far," but it is only a method or an orientation (P 32).

Now, statements such as these raise troublesome questions. In general, it should be pointed out that James is claiming for pragmatism elements found in a wide variety of philosophic methodologies without completely identifying it with any one of them. The nervous issue for the realist–nominalist debate is his insistence on particulars. A classic text cited by his critics is the one found in *The Meaning of Truth* where he repeats and attempts to explain a statement made in an earlier address in which he described pragmatism as holding that "the meaning of any proposition can always be brought down to some particular consequence, in our future practical experience, whether active or passive." He adds a qualifying phrase: "the point lying rather in the fact that the experience must be particular, than in the fact that it must be active," where "active" means "practical" in the narrow sense (MT

279). Now, in this section James is answering the charge that pragmatism has no theoretic interests. He calls this "an absolutely wanton slander" and "rubbish," though he admits that his use of the word practical was sometimes careless.[15] This led to the charge that practical was opposed to the genuinely cognitive and that truth depended not on any objective reality or on any other truth but solely on the satisfaction resulting from the solution of a momentary, particular perplexity. James, of course, rejects this interpretation of pragmatism but at the same time he sees no contradiction between particular consequences and theory. Our great interest is in consistency, which means that what truths we hold now will obtain on other occasions. It is for this reason that we continually compare truth with truth, we ask if belief in a present or past fact will hold up in the future. This can be ascertained by returning to particular facts to see if the belief will again be verified. This is consistent with his view that, while we do hold firm beliefs, each one must "pass muster," that is, it is an hypothesis subject to verification, alteration, or rejection in the light of future experience.

But underlying his insistence on the return to experience is James's conviction that there are "common-sense traditions" by which we live and which at first were discovered by "an inductive generalization." Among others, we accept the idea of classes and sub-classes and the distinction *between fortuitous and regularly caused connections*. This gives shareable and manageable shape to what would be a chaos of individual experiences. We can therefore predict the course of future experience, communicate with others, and guide our lives by rule (MT 208). This view agrees very well with the very meaning of belief. James shares with Peirce the conviction that belief is a rule or habit of action whereby we expect certain reactions when confronted with a given fact or object. If we did not think that objects acted and reacted in consistent ways, a rule or habit would never develop. James states that mental habits are formed "where the same objects, or the *same kinds of objects*, recur and *follow 'law.'*" And because this is so, the mind experiences intellectual satisfaction when expectations are realized and dissatisfaction when they are not (MT 224).

One more piece of evidence cited by James's critics as an indication of his individualism is his failure to insist that the process of inquiry, test, and verification must be a public, community enterprise. This criticism has some validity if we compare James with Peirce on this point. Surely Peirce insisted that inquiry was to be carried out by a community of scholars, putting their work into the public forum and sharing procedures and results (CP 2.157). James did not exclude all this, though he did not dwell on it. But there is one passage that ought not to be ignored. He is answering those who criticize the pragmatists' notion of "opinion" and its relation to truth. They seem to think that opinion is limited to its dictionary meaning, which defines it as "what some one thinks or believes." Opinion then signifies what an *individual* thinks without any relation to what may be true. From this James draws the absurd conclusion that an opinion held by one person would have equal standing with an opinion held in common by a billion others. In opposition to this, James argues that by opinion the pragmatist means assumptions which are simple inductions derived from ordinary past experience and projected into the future. By social communication humans reach a consensus that such opinions have worked successfully and have been verified many times over. Furthermore, some people are better qualified to form solid opinions by reason of their relative ability, wider experience, and expertise. In forming opinions, we ought "to compare notes, discuss, and follow the opinion of our betters." It follows that the opinion which the pragmatist has in mind is not opinion in the abstract, removed from the give-and-take of public comparison and intercommunication. It is then and only then that "absolute truth" can be described as "an ideal set of formulations toward which all opinion may in the long run of experience be expected to converge" (MT 309; P 106-107).

As a final note, references can be made to the relation between the realism–nominalism debate and James's radical empiricism. In the previous chapter, it was shown that James held for connections not only between ideas but also between objects. In the context he did not explicitly propose his empiricism in opposition to nominalism. The main attack was directed against idealism's world of disconnected objects, but it applies equally to the atomism of classical empiricism and nominalism. Just as pragmatic belief presupposes the reality of objective connections acting in lawlike and predictable ways, so radical empiricism is based on the same assumptions. In short, the pragmatic theory of belief and James's radical empiricism are incompatible with both classical empiricism and contemporary nominalism. Or putting it in another way: they presuppose that objects in nature act in regular ways according to a rule or law, independently of what you or I or anyone else thinks about it.

DEWEY

In a recent book, Ralph Sleeper claimed that, in casting his lot with realism as against idealism, Dewey did not espouse either the fixed and universal essences of Peirce or the extreme pluralism of James. Instead he veered toward the latter "without going all the way."[16] In my own view, Sleeper has criticized Peirce's synechism and Scotistic realism without sufficiently taking into account his developmental evolutionism. At the same time, he reads James as moving toward an extreme pluralism "in which almost everything goes."[17] In the preceding pages, I have tried, indirectly at least, to counter both these interpretations.

But that leaves us with the question as to where Dewey stands on the topic of this chapter. Sleeper has ably documented the development of Dewey's logic as an alternative to idealism and relativism, so there is no need to rehearse that story again. Though I would question Sleeper's tendency to view logic as *the* key to understanding Dewey, it is without doubt an important way into his thought and it is the one which I shall highlight in the present discussion. In the opening sentences of *Essays in Experimental Logic*, Dewey states that what he has to say about the temporal development of experience is the key to understanding the essays contained in that book (MW 10:320). In *Reconstruction in Philosophy*, he defines logic as the clarified and systematized set of procedures by which the reconstruction of experience can be efficiently carried out (MW 12:157). By the temporal development and reconstruction of experience, Dewey means the ongoing growth of the human person in a changing universe. Logic, then, had a central role in all the topics that he discussed—education, morals, religion, art, social and political theory. In *Experience and Nature*, he described the world in which we live as precarious, perilous, hazardous, uncertain. There are indeed stabilities, joys, occasions of happiness, but the reality of misfortune and tragedy tends to become more imperious, demanding a solution. It is this mixture of stability and uncertainty that gives rise to philosophy, which in this context means the development of intellectual procedures, a logic of inquiry, by which human beings can find satisfactory solutions to problems that affect them in all areas of life (LW 1:43–46). If this be the case, claims Dewey, then logic must avoid two extremes. It ought not exclude the truth of subject matter and confine itself purely to formal laws of correct thinking. Nor should it look upon the universe as embodying rigid thought structures to which reasoning must conform. So insistent is his view of logic as directly related to life's situations that he gave the back-of-the-hand to a whole array of philosophers. Aristotle, for one, made a good start in recognizing contingencies but unfortunately gave the preference to the fixed and certain. Kant assigned all that is manifold to sense and all that is uniform and permanent to reason. In one sweeping statement, Dewey indicts a whole group of philosophers for dividing the character of existence into a superior true realm and a lower, illusory, insignificant realm; among these he includes Plato, Democritus, St. Thomas Aquinas, Spinoza, Aristotle, Kant, Descartes, Comte, Haeckel, and Mrs. Eddy (LW 1:55)! Following Peirce, but with more direct application to specific human problems, Dewey maintains in *Reconstruction in Philosophy* that thinking begins with specific troubles that arise in the course of daily experience. Doubt and perplexity arise and a solution is sought. An idea is formed as the best means of settling doubt and enabling the inquiry to reach once more a settled condition. Ideas at best are hypotheses to be tested in experience; they are not theories or systems settled once for all according to some preconceived pattern dictating how one must think (MW 12:159–61).

In *Logic: The Theory of Inquiry*, Dewey asserts that the settled state of affairs achieved through active engagement with the facts constitutes belief, which he calls "warranted assertability." Belief is also a "doubled-barreled" word; it refers both to the state of mind that is relieved of the tension of doubt and also to objective reality. Dewey does not hesitate to call belief by the term *knowledge*, provided it is not taken to signify something fixed or eternal. In turn, logic must not be subordinated to "metaphysical and epistemological conditions" which would isolate it from changing situations and reduce it to rigid formulations (LW 12:14–16). Though belief or knowledge and the logical process by which it is achieved are open-ended, logic for Dewey can still be called "normative" and "regulative." To say that experience merely informs us how people have thought or do think while logic dictates how they should think is "ludicrously inept." In fact, logic combines both. Improved and refined processes of inquiry enable us to distinguish between success and failure and to eliminate flagrant cases of the latter. These same processes can then be used as directives for future inquiry. But again norms are not "external canons" to which inquiry must rigidly adhere. They are, rather, self-correcting processes that are themselves subject to new tests in the light of future experience (LW 12:13–14). Further, the criteria for inquiry are empirical, since they arise from the very process of inquiry. But that does not mean that they lack "rational standing." They give directives as to the means to be used to achieve projected consequences, but they are not to be taken as fixed premises. In Dewey's view, reasonableness or rationality had been "hypostatized" and looked upon as a faculty intuitively grasping first principles that are evident and self-verifying. Instead reasonableness involves the relation of means that have the greatest possibility of attaining intended ends and progressively stable beliefs. Consequently postulates or first principles are not denied; on the contrary, they are indispensable if inquiry is to proceed efficiently. But they arise from the very process of inquiry itself and are not *a priori* principles, fixed before inquiry begins or setting its conditions from the outside (LW 12:17–21).

With this as background, it is now possible to address the question regarding Dewey's position on necessity and causality. Regarding the first, it is obvious that he would not accept necessity in any fixed or rigid sense. But at same time we can classify objects and generalized procedures on the assumption that objects in the world act in regular ways, even though there is no absolute guarantee that the same objects will always act in precisely the same way. In *Reconstruction*, Dewey uses the analogy of making one's way through unfamiliar territory; he likens classification to the process of changing bewildering byways in experience into a familiar series of roads that make possible transportation and communication in experience (MW 12:166–69). A necessary condition for this is that there be uniformities in nature. Without them, predictability and science itself would be impossible. Correlative to this and on the subjective side is the notion of beliefs as habits of action. In *Logic*, he states that these are formed because objects in nature act in uniform ways, and inquiry leads to successful consequences. Habits may then be called rules, laws, or principles of action, and the formulations that express these will constitute logical principles of all inquiries. They have been found to lead to sound conclusions in the past so that they can be accepted as regulating further inquiry, at least until reasons arise for calling them into question (LW 12: 20–21).

Summing up Dewey's position, it can be seen that, instead of using the term necessity, he prefers to speak about the regular ways in which objects act and react in nature. They are reliable enough for general formulations as to how things have acted in the past, for predictions regarding their future action, and for belief or habits of action in dealing with nature. But with Peirce and James, he opts for a world that is plastic, malleable, and changeable, and that excludes fixed and invariable regularities.

It remains now to examine Dewey's position on causation. This is discussed in Chapter XXII of *Logic: The Theory of Inquiry*, entitled "Scientific Law—Causation and Sequences." He begins by citing John Stuart Mill's view of scientific laws as "formulations of uniform and unconditional sequences of events" (LW 12:437). The obvious objection to this approach is that the relations between singular instances are incapable of supplying the ground and content for the necessary and unconditional sequences that are claimed to exist between and among these sequences. And yet some aspects of Mill's view seem to be valid. The scientific method does have recourse to necessary universal propositions. If these propositions are applied to abstract, non-existential content, there is little cause for complaint. But if they are taken as expressions of individual existential instances, it becomes evident that an examination of the empirical data fails to yield the same kind of necessity as that which is embodied in the abstract universal proposition (LW 12:438–40). It is this latter problem that Dewey attempts to solve in his discussion of "causal laws."

Dewey's initial move is to re-examine what is meant by cause.

these were admitted, the way would be open to an interpretation of the universe as operating in regular ways according to some overarching finality. Also influencing his position was his rejection of idealistic forms of logic which dictated how one ought to think about reality. Consequently he reserved causality to "ends-in-view," that is, to human intelligence using means for the attainment of projected goals.

And yet, Dewey was surely aware that intelligent action presupposes that objects act in regular and predictable ways; otherwise such action would be haphazard and subject to chance. Such suppositions are essential also for his theory of belief as a habit of action. But he stopped short of giving existential grounding for causation beyond the fact that things are linked in a unity of sequences. He did not seem to realize that this undercut his clear statement that logic is regulative and has rational standing since it directs future action based on the fact that objects in the universe will continue to act in regular and ordered ways. If causal relations are viewed merely as sequences, there is danger that rationality or reasonableness will be imposed on nature, a move which Dewey himself fought so hard to reject. He also failed to understand that Peirce's synechism and Scotistic realism were not a return to fixed and unchanging essences of the kind so strongly opposed by empiricists and pragmatists alike but rather a modification of these in terms of evolution. Peirce himself had stated that, though he was strongly influenced by Scotus, the latter's logic and metaphysics should not be slavishly worshipped but be adapted to modern culture (CP 1.6). Nor did he appreciate James's serious though not entirely successful attempt to account for change and process without reverting to a sheer relativism. Finally, to reduce Dewey's meaning of necessity to that which is required as means for attainment of projected ends is a weak if not equivocal use of the word *necessity*. Sleeper has made a good textual case for arguing that this is all that Dewey meant.[18] I personally believe that, without being aware of it, Dewey meant more than that; otherwise belief, the logical process as normative, and the very underpinning of "ends-in-view" are seriously eroded. But that, I suppose, is one of the many issues that can be debated in any interpretation of Dewey's thought.

NOTES

1. On the influence of Boyle's corpuscular theory of matter on Locke, see John W. Yolton, *Locke and the Compass of Human Understanding* (Cambridge: Cambridge University Press, 1970), chap. 1, esp. pp. 79–80.

2. The abbreviation EN refers to Hume's *Enquiries Concerning Human Understanding* and *Concerning the Principles of Morals.* All references to the two *Enquiries* are included in the text as EN1 and EN2 with page number.

3. Of course, Hume held that certainty through a comparison of ideas could be attained by both intuition and demonstrative reasoning. But "the most general and most popular explication" for the existence of powers was through reasoning. See T 157. Hence he focused his criticism on demonstrative reasoning and rejected it as incapable of establishing the existence of powers.

4. Cited in Norman Kemp Smith, *The Philosophy of David Hume* (New York: St. Martin's, 1964), p. 443.

5. But as opposed to Hume, Peirce would deny that these events, if taken in isolation, could be understood or even be called real. In short, there are no isolated, atomic events. Put positively: all things are related in a system, grouped according to general laws. This is an aspect of Peirce's synechism. See CP 1.424.

6. Vincent G. Potter, S.J., *Charles S. Peirce: On Norms and Ideals* (Amherst: University of Massachusetts Press, 1969), pp. 92 and 98. See also CP 5.48 and 5.425. Peirce calls a general a Third.

7. Attempts have been made to show that we are directly aware of the actions of causal powers. See, for example, R. Harré and E. H. Madden, *Causal Powers: A Theory of Natural Necessity* (Oxford: Blackwell, 1975), esp. pp. 49–67. Though these authors argue cogently against a Humean atomistic account of active causality, I do not think that they have convincingly sustained their main thesis.

8. Manley Thompson, "Peirce's Experimental Proof of Scholastic Realism," in *Studies in the Philosophy of Charles Sanders Peirce*, Second Series, edd. Edward C. Moore and Richard S. Robin (Amherst: University of Massachusetts Press, 1964), pp. 414–29.

9. Ibid., pp. 416–17.

10. Harré and Madden, *Causal Powers*, pp. 27–28.

11. T. E. Jessop, "Some Misunderstandings of Hume," *Hume: A Collection of Critical Essays*, ed. V. C. Chappell (Garden City, N.Y.: Doubleday, 1966), p. 52.

12. A fuller treatment of Peirce's thought would have to consider the theory of evolution, fallibilism, belief, and truth. All these concepts are

complex and have difficulties of their own. However, in limiting myself to real powers and their justification, I have addressed some of the main issues concerning the problem of necessary connection.

13. W. B. Gallie, *Peirce and Pragmatism* (Harmondsworth: Penguin, 1952), p. 29.

14. Thomas S. Knight, *Charles Peirce* (New York: Washington Square, 1965), p. 61.

15. Unfortunately James's further explanation is not always as careful as it should be.

16. Ralph W. Sleeper, *The Necessity of Pragmatism: John Dewey's Conception of Philosophy* (New Haven: Yale University Press, 1986), p. 69 and note 23.

17. Ibid.

18. Ibid., pp. 35–40 and passim.

3

PERSONAL IDENTITY

ON ANY LIST OF PHILOSOPHICAL ISSUES that were affected by the rise of empiricism after Descartes, one of the first would have to be the question of person or personal identity. The main reason was that empiricism, beginning with Locke, called into question the idea and the reality of substance as an enduring source or substrate of successive mental states. Once this move was made, empiricists had to propose an alternative philosophical explanation for the meaning of person. It is the task of this chapter to trace the development of this move as it worked its way through the British empiricists and American pragmatists.

LOCKE

Locke's theory of person is developed in the *Essay*, Book II, Chapter XXVII, entitled "Identity and Diversity." The chapter is lengthy, even wordy, repetitious, complex, and somewhat ambiguous, yet it is filled with subtle distinctions and nuances. Many notions are included: namely, substance, person, personal identity, soul, thinking, body, man. My own attempt to represent these notions and to put them into some kind of coherent form is tentative and perhaps highly personal. In the process I shall occasionally depart from the order of development as given in the *Essay*.

At the outset, it would be well to review Locke's meaning of substance. This has already been discussed in the first chapter of this volume. As for substance in general, we have no idea of it save as some substrate in which our simple ideas subsist. Particular substances are combinations of simple ideas. An idea of corporeal substance is made up of the qualities which we acquire through the senses; the idea of immaterial substance, spirit, or mind is a combination of such operations as thinking and willing. We have no clear or distinct idea of either of these kinds of substance. Further, though the precise nature of body is unknown to us, we do have clear, distinct ideas of two primary or original qualities or properties of body, namely, a thing composed of solid, coherent, extended, separable parts and capable of moving other bodies. Figure can be included in this list, but it is a consequence of finite extension. Locke calls body a "thing" but it is clear that he means a supposed "something" as a support for these qualities, though we have no clear, distinct idea of that support. Two primary activities are attributed to immaterial or spiritual substance, which is called spirit, soul, or mind. These activities are thinking and the power of moving one's own body. Thinking includes a wide variety of activities, such as reasoning, understanding, meditating, believing, doubting, fearing, hoping, willing, intending, seeing, hearing, smelling, tasting, feeling. Again, Locke refers often to immaterial substance as a being or thing, though it too must be understood as a name for a collection of activities and does not designate any being of which we have a clear or distinct idea. He maintains that we are convinced that solid, extended substances and thinking ones exist; the former we know by sensation and the latter by reflection. But we do not know the nature, causes, or manner of existing of these substances (EU 296–97, 305–14, 335).

Locke recognizes that there are problems regarding immaterial substances or spirits. The idea of these originally arises from the fact that we reason that the operations of the mind do not subsist of themselves, and we cannot understand how they can belong to body or can be produced by it (EU 297). We conclude, therefore, that spirits exist. If this seems difficult to accept, he reminds us that the notion of body has difficulties too—for example, the divisibility *ad infinitum* of any finite extended object. This is even harder to understand and seems to entail a greater absurdity than the idea of an immaterial knowing substance. Further, since we have clear, distinct, and separate ideas of both thinking and solidity, there is no reason to doubt that thinking can exist without solidity and vice versa (EU 313–14).

Later in the *Essay*, when discussing the extent of human knowledge, Locke returns to the notion of immaterial substance. He acknowledges that we cannot achieve the certainty of demonstrative proof about its existence. Further, he concedes that there are solid arguments for the soul being either unextended substance or thinking extended matter. He seems to feel, however, that the reasons in favor of immaterial substance are more persuasive than those against it, though he does not develop a philosophical argument for his position. In the last analysis, he maintains that, in the present state of knowledge, we must in this case as in many others be content with faith and probability instead of unassailable proofs. He assures himself that, even without such proof, the ends of morality and religion are sufficiently safeguarded. For all that, there is no doubt that there is in us something that thinks, for the very doubt we have about its nature confirms the certainty of its existence (EU 541–43).

With this as background, it is now possible to consider Locke's meaning of person. And here he makes a subtle distinction between an act of thinking, such as smelling, tasting, feeling, meditating, and willing, and the consciousness or awareness of performing such acts. It is this consciousness, which is inseparable from thinking, that constitutes the self. In the very act of thinking, we are conscious of doing so, "and by this every one is to himself, that which he calls *self*" (EU 35). This consciousness constitutes the self and distinguishes one self from all others. This is called personal identity, that is, the sameness of a rational being. The identity of that person goes back as far as consciousness can be traced to any previous act or acts of thinking. If a present consciousness, aware of its present act, is also conscious of performing an act in the past, then it is the same self in both instances.

Once Locke has identified person as awareness of an act of thinking, some intriguing consequences follow. For one thing, since personal identity depends only on one and the same consciousness, identical substance is not essential for identity of person. It is not inconceivable that a present consciousness, aware not only of a present action but also of past actions, could be successively in two different substances. In that case there would not be two persons but one, even though separated in time and existing in two different substances, just as a man is the same after a change of clothes or after a long or short sleep. So, too, two different thinking substances could be the same person. On the other hand, given this meaning of person, it is not impossible that the same immaterial substance could be two different persons. On this hypothesis, the same substance would be deprived of all consciousness of past actions and would begin anew, as it were. Although the same individual *substance* would remain, there would be a different *self* (EU 335–39).

Locke also considers the relation of person and soul to the body. He draws a distinction between self and man. The identity of the same man consists in the continuance of the same life of the soul or spirit that remains amid the constant but gradual addition and loss of the particles that constitute a living body. For Locke, then, body is essential for constituting a man (EU 331–32, 335). But it must be a body of a certain figure. He admits that it is difficult to set definite criteria for deciding what constitutes a human body, simply because we do not know real but only nominal essences. At times it may be difficult to tell whether a fetus is a monster or a human (EU 453–55). But he is quite clear as to what kinds of bodies should be excluded. Thus if it could be ascertained that the soul of Heliogabalus entered one of his hogs, no one would call it a man or Heliogabalus (EU 332). Or if a cat or a parrot began to reason, speak, or philosophize, one would not call it a man but an intelligent, rational cat or parrot. Conversely, if a man were bereft of reason all his life, we would not call him an animal but a dull, irrational man (EU 333). Again, if the soul of a prince, with the consciousness of all the past actions of the prince, were to enter the body of a cobbler, he would be the same person as the prince, even though people would take him, as a man, to be a cobbler. Locke admits that in the popular view spirit, man, and person are the same. But on further reflection and inquiry, this is seen not to be the case (EU 340). Given these distinctions, Locke conjures up other bizarre possibilities. If I had the consciousness that I saw Noah's ark and the flood and also the overflowing of the Thames during the past winter, then the I who am conscious of writing now would be the same self. Or suppose that the same spiritual soul that was in the body of Nestor or Thersites at the siege of Troy were to continue to the present, with the gradual change of bodily particles that takes place in the ordinary life of a human being; suppose further that at present the soul has no consciousness of any of the past actions of Nestor or Thersites; would it be the same person or self? On Locke's principles, it would not, since person extends only as far as consciousness (EU 339). Or again, since self is determined, not by identity of substance, but by identity of consciousness, if two different incommunicable consciousnesses alternately inhabited the same individual soul and body by day and night, there would be two persons (EU 344–45).

The detail, complexity, and at times repetitiveness of Locke's discussion are enough to set one's head spinning. But through it all it is clear that substance, person, and man are not the same, that man includes soul and a relation to a body (though this relationship is not detailed), and that it is not impossible to have successively multiple persons in a single substance or body as well as one person in several substances or bodies. The fundamental reason is that for Locke person is not an abiding entity nor thinking nor willing but *consciousness* of thinking or willing, even though, as it actually exists, it is somehow related to a body that is at least generally identifiable as human.

The crucial move is Locke's claim that we have no clear, distinct idea of substance as an abiding principle of being and activity. Consequently, substance cannot serve as the link from one stage of consciousness, or from one period of time, to another. Consciousness of performing acts of thinking and willing is taken to be person and is continuous only as far back as consciousness itself can reach. But he does not explain precisely how consciousness can extend itself back in time or what the limits of its duration are. There is indeed some carry-over of self from one moment to another, but at times it seems quite short-lived, at other times quite extended. Surprisingly he does not highlight the role of memory. It seems to be supposed, otherwise how explain the fact that a present consciousness can extend back to past conscious states? At one point, he does use the terms *memory* and *recollection* as the source of the unification of conscious states. But he does not develop this further (EU 344–45). There is one move, however, that Locke does not make. He does not explicitly reduce person to a series of discrete, disconnected perceptions, as Hume will later attempt to do. On one important point, Locke's position is especially fuzzy. It is the question of culpability for past actions which have been forgotten and cannot be retrieved. He mentions this as a possible objection against his own position. He grants that on his own principles distinct incommunicable consciousnesses at different times constitute different persons. Humane laws recognize this when they do not punish a sane man for actions done in a moment of insanity. This seems sound enough. But then, what about crimes done when one is drunk? Locke adds that "in the great day" no one will be punished for acts which were not conscious, and so any mistakes made in the application of the law in this life will be rectified (EU 342–43). Such an answer, while perhaps consoling for those who believe in a hereafter, is highly dubious as a principle for dealing with the complexities of such kinds of actions in this life.

In all these examples, Locke is giving situations which are possible or which at least are not inconceivable, given his notion of person. In the end, he holds as more probable the opinion that consciousness is connected with the activity of one material substance. He is also ready to admit that his views will look strange and that they may indeed be such. Yet they are not absurd in view of our limited knowledge of the thinking subject (EU 345, 347). It was left to Hume to sweep aside the ambiguities in Locke's position and explicitly to locate personal identity in successive discrete perceptions.

HUME AND JAMES

William James once wrote that, since Hume's time, the problem of personal identity has been "the most puzzling puzzle with which psychology has to deal" and the most controversial (PP 314). The situation has not changed much since that statement was made almost a century ago; if anything, the puzzle has become even more complex. It is also the case that Hume and James are two philosophers who would have to be considered in any contemporary discussion of personal identity. This is not to say that either one has definitively resolved the puzzle, but they have identified the main areas of the debate and have come to grips with some of the central issues. Consequently the purpose of this section is to examine and evaluate in turn the positions of Hume and James on personal identity. In the process I hope to show that, while James went further than Hume in developing a coherent theory, it is in the last analysis basically flawed at crucial points.

Hume begins his discussion by indicating the problem that concerns him: namely, the continued existence of the self. Some philosophers assert that we are at every moment intimately conscious of what we call our self. It is a datum of immediate consciousness that gives certainty beyond that of a demonstration. Hume denies this claim. He maintains that it goes counter to the very experience which is invoked to justify the conviction. His main objection is that we do not have any idea of self simply because there is no corresponding impression. His starting point of knowledge demands that every idea have some one impression. The impression of self would have to remain invariably the same throughout our lives, for that is the way the self is supposed to exist. But there is no such impression; we are conscious only of a series of impressions, such as pain and pleasure, grief and joy, passions and sensations which succeed one another and never exist permanently. Moreover the perceptions that succeed one another are all different, distinguishable, and separable from each other. What I call myself is merely some particular perception. Hume immediately moves to the further affirmation that self is simply a bundle or collection of different perceptions that quickly pass by in succession. This, Hume maintains, is evident through reflection; in sight our eyes can vary our perceptions merely by turning in different directions. This is confirmed in all our thoughts, senses, and faculties. And through it all, there is no one power of the soul that remains unchanged even for a single moment (T 252–53).

And yet, just as in his treatment of causation and the continued existence of external objects, Hume asks what great "propension" prompts us to attribute identity to these successive perceptions and to conclude to a continued existing self. He sharpens the question by clarifying more fully the nature of the difficulty. It consists precisely in the fact that we are confronted with a contradiction between identity and diversity. On the one hand, we have a distinct idea of something that remains unchanged and uninterrupted through time, and this idea is called identity or sameness. At the same time, we have a distinct idea of several different objects succeeding one another though linked by a relation, and this is an idea of diversity. Although these ideas of identity and diversity are perfectly distinct and contrary, they are confounded one with the other in our minds. This confusion is due to two acts of the imagination, one accounting for identity and the other for diversity, and these acts have almost the same feeling. The reason why we substitute the notion of identity for that of diversity is the resemblance that exists between the objects. This is in reality a confusion and a mistake. Our propensity to repeat this state of affairs is so great that we do so inadvertently. On reflection, we correct this mistake but the bias of imagination to this absurdity proves to be too strong. We end up by feigning the continued existence of the perceptions of our senses and we invent the notion of soul, self, or substance, or at least we imagine something unknown and mysterious that connects the various parts together (T 253–54).

Further on, Hume considers in a more formal way the basic reason why we identify distinct perceptions (T 259–62). He recalls a position which he had already developed, namely, that the three principles in the ideal world which prompt the imagination to unite ideas are resemblance, contiguity, and causation. Identity depends on these. He dismisses contiguity as not applicable, probably because many perceptions that we attribute to a contin-ued self are in fact not contiguous, though many are. A perception I had last week is not contiguous with a present one, though an immediately preceding one surely is. But the second relation, resemblance, may apply in all cases, and it plays a leading role, as he has already indicated. He now explains it further. Given a succession of perceptions, an individual remembers many that are past. Memory frequently brings back images of past perceptions that resemble one another, and the imagination moves easily from one to another, making all of them seem to be one continuous object. Memory both discovers identity and contributes to its emergence by giving rise to a relation of resemblance among the perceptions (T 260–61).

From resemblance, Hume moves to causation. There is a rela-tion of cause and effect which links into a system the different perceptions or different existences. Impressions give rise to corresponding ideas and these in turn to other impressions in a constant succession. Hume concludes by emphasizing memory as the principal source of personal identity just as he did in his treatment of resemblance. Memory alone makes us aware of the continuance and extent of the succession of perceptions. Without it, we could not achieve the notion of causation or the sequence of causes and effects which self or person constitute. We can then extend the chain of causes and identity of our persons even to times, circumstances, and actions that we have forgotten but suppose to have existed. Memory reveals the relation of cause and effect among our different perceptions. From this description it can be seen that Hume, much more than Locke, gives memory a prominent place in his theory of personal identity (T 261–62).

There are three points in the above account which merit further consideration: Hume's attempt to explain what the self is, and his application of the two relations of resemblance and causation to personal identity. The first has to do with his own rendition of what he takes the self to be. Appealing to his own consciousness when he enters intimately into what he calls the self, he claims to find nothing but a particular perception. Some lines later, he calls the self nothing but a bundle or collection of different perceptions. A difficulty immediately arises. One could ask *who* or *what* it is that is aware of a single perception or that unites the various perceptions into a bundle or collection. It does not help to invoke imagination or memory, for the question recurs: Who or what imagines or remembers? Perhaps another perception? If so, who or what perceives? And so on, *ad infinitum*.

The second point, resemblance, is found in a passage that is brief and far from clear. At the outset, it is reasonable to suppose that Hume is talking about resemblance as a natural relation, not a philosophical one. The former is a quality found in ideas because of their similarity and is the reason why imagination moves easily from one idea to any other that resembles it (T 11). Resemblance as a philosophical relation is much broader. In a sense any two things can be said to resemble each other if we try hard enough to find some point of comparison (T 14). For example (mine, not Hume's), one could say that the idea of a stone resembles that of a feather because both objects are material. But then the imagination would not readily go from one to the other.

In this regard, it should be noted that Hume first takes up the notions of resemblance and association early in the *Treatise* (I, I, iv & v). There he is speaking about resemblance and association between ideas. Regarding personal identity, however, the term he commonly uses is perception, which is wider than idea and seems to include any conscious state. What, then, is the nature of the resemblance? Perhaps the perceptions resemble one another simply by being perceptions of a particular kind. But this does not seem plausible since Hume has not indicated what characteristics are common to all perceptions or in what way they sometimes resemble one another and sometimes do not. Perhaps, then, there is a resemblance regarding the kinds of perceptions. It could be granted that some perceptions bear such a resemblance, as is the case when I look successively at a number of trees. The resemblance begins to blur if the perceptions that run in succession are those of a tree, a building, and a mountain. The resemblance breaks down completely when the perceptions are the image of a tree, the taste of an orange, the sound of thunder, and the pain of a toothache. In brief, the use that Hume makes of resemblance is unclear.

Perhaps greater clarity can be found in Hume's discussion of causation, for it is a central element in his whole philosophy. But again his treatment is even more ambiguous than that of resemblance. He states in a general and vague way that the relation of cause and effect provides the link among perceptions which "mutually produce, destroy, influence, and modify each other." Impressions give rise to ideas which produce other impressions. "One thought chaces another, and draws after it a third, by which it is expell'd in its turn" (T 261). I can find no more vague or less satisfying passage in all of Hume's writings. He has already given a long and careful account of cause and effect, running through resemblance, contiguity, constant conjunction, custom, habit, impression of reflection, to the idea of necessary connection. All this is familiar to the student of Hume. But here his customary careful and meticulous approach to problems deserts him. He could have shown in brief fashion how the fundamental principles are applied to personal identity. Instead he gives a hurried statement that causation accounts for personal identity without explaining how this is so.

There is even a more glaring weakness here. Not only did Hume fail to show how causation applies to personal identity but he could not have formulated a consistent position even if he had tried. There is an element essential to the cause-and-effect relationship that is missing in the succession of perceptions. That element is constant conjunction. Barry Stroud has pointed this out very well.

> In order for each of my perceptions to be both the effect of some and the cause of others of my perceptions, each of my perceptions would have to belong to a class of perceptions the members of which have been constantly conjoined with members of those classes of perceptions to which its immediate predecessor and its immediate successor belong. Any stretch of experience ABCDE-FGHIJKL would have to be such that, for example, H is caused by G (or by every perception up to and including G). And on Hume's theory that implies that there is a constant conjunction between perceptions like G (or like ABCDEFG) and perceptions like H. Only if there were such conjunctions would we come to think of the two as causally connected. But our experience in fact exhibits no such regularities. It is not true that we get an experience of a certain sort only when we have just had an experience of a certain other sort, or that experiences of the first sort are always followed by experiences of another sort. Our experience does not exhibit such uniformities.[1]

Stroud concedes that there are some causal connections between perceptions—for example, those taking place between impressions and their corresponding ideas. But the case is different when I look at a tree and then a building, for the first perception is not the cause of the second either in fact or in accordance with Hume's own theory of causation. Consequently his theory of causality falls apart and cannot serve, on his own terms, to explain personal identity. Hume's last resort is memory as the chief source of personal identity (T 261). Whether he means that it stands alone or must be taken along with causation, he does not explicitly say, though the latter is more likely. In the end, as we know, Hume acknowledged that the final explanation of personal identity was beyond him, though he thought it possible that he himself or others might one day arrive at a satisfactory position (T 636).

It is precisely this task that James assumes.[2] In Chapter 1 we saw how he opposed Hume's description of consciousness. Basically he charged that Hume made an incomplete and even erroneous reflection on our mental states. While Hume described consciousness as a sequence of discrete particles, James maintained that it is continuous. It should be mentioned that so far James has engaged in introspective observation to describe how consciousness *feels*. In doing so, he claims to come up with a theory that sharply contrasts with the Humean perspective. Not only that, he argues that such faulty introspection of consciousness can also distort our awareness of the self. He quotes at length the passage in which Hume proposes his theory of personal identity (T 251–53). He acknowledges Hume's fine introspective work in showing how great the consciousness of diversity really is. But Hume then pours out the baby with the bath, for he holds that the self is reduced to abstract and absolute diversity (T 352). He fails to realize that unity is just as much a part of consciousness as diversity. This view of consciousness affects Hume's theory of personal identity. James refers to the Appendix of the *Treatise* (T 636) which states that all distinct perceptions are distinct existences and the mind is never aware of any real connections between them. Hume leaves out the "judging thought" and dismisses any thread of resemblance or sameness. There is no alternative between unity and separateness (T 352).

To James, this description of self is false. Introspective observation shows that "every thought is a part of a personal consciousness" (PP 220). Thought is not left hanging in mid-air.

> It seems as if the elementary psychic fact were not *thought* or *this thought*, but *my thought*, every thought being owned. . . . On these terms the personal self rather than the thought might be treated as the immediate datum in psychology. The universal conscious fact is not 'feeling and thought exist,' but 'I think' and 'I feel.' No psychology, at any rate, can question the *existence* of personal selves [PP 221].

This means that the very state of consciousness is permeated with the marks of a unified personality and that the self need not be introduced from the outside.

The same can be said even when there is a time-gap in consciousness as happens, for example, when one wakes from sleep. In one sense, consciousness is interrupted. But in another sense it is continuous and unified because the parts are inwardly connected. And why is this so? Simply because the parts belong to a common whole which is called I, myself, or me. Consciousness before the time-gap and consciousness after it feel as if they belonged together as parts of the same self (PP 231–32). James describes further the characteristics causing the feeling of a common whole. He gives an example of the conscious state of Peter when he wakes from sleep and remembers his last state.

> Remembrance is like direct feeling; its object is suffused with a warmth and intimacy to which no object or mere conception ever attains. This quality of warmth and intimacy and immediacy is what Peter's present thought also possesses for itself. So sure as this present is me, is mine, it says, so sure is anything else that comes with the same warmth and intimacy and immediacy, me and mine. What the qualities called warmth and intimacy may in themselves be will have to be matter for future consideration. But whatever past feelings appear with those qualities must be admitted to receive the greeting of the present mental state, to be owned by it, and accepted as belonging together with it in a common self. This community of self is what the time-gap cannot break in twain, and is why a present thought, although not ignorant of the time gap, can still regard itself as continuous with certain chosen portions of the past [PP 232–33].

James contrasts this version of consciousness with that of the associationists. The latter attempt to explain the unity of thought by a bundle of separate ideas, with the result that they must add an Ego to the bundle to unify it and relate the various ideas with one another. For James, internal to consciousness is the feeling of unity and continuity in a common self (PP 267).

So far, I have examined James's account of introspective observation inasmuch as it reveals that we have a *feeling* of unity as well as diversity in our conscious states and also a *feeling* of personal identity. In reality these are not two feelings but one. So important is the feeling that without it thought could not even take place. Now James brings us to the central problem. It can be stated as follows. Personal identity definitely exists as a *feeling*, but does it exist as a *fact*? The psychologist must now play the part of the critic and see whether consciousness is correct or not in asserting that the self of yesterday is the same as that of today. James first recalls the qualities of warmth and intimacy which are characteristics of past and present selves. He then introduces his famous example of the herd of cattle let loose for the winter on some prairie. At the spring roundup the owner gathers all the animals bearing his particular brand. The herd-mark is like a thread through a chaplet drawing into a unit parts that may differ among themselves. So, too, distant selves appear as continuous with the self of the present moment because they all bear the mark of warmth and intimacy. Like Hume, James uses the word "resemblance" but he means a resemblance in the sensible characteristics of perceptions. Thus continuity overcomes the separateness of discontinuity and similarity the discreteness of discontinuity (PP 316–19).

But the account is not complete. Common sense is not satisfied with a mere appearance of similarity or continuity; it insists that there is "a real belonging to a real Owner," a real self. The herd of cattle requires more than a brand to bring them together. There must also be an owner, a *self*-brand beyond a herd-brand. It is the fact of belonging to the owner that is the reason for the branding, not the other way around. The owner furnishes a real center and the animals stay together by staying with him. So, too, in the case of the self, common sense insists that there be a real proprietor; otherwise there would be no unity in personal consciousness (PP 319–20).

James pushes his analysis further. He has accounted for the unity among past and present selves. There is a self, an owner. But James rejects any substantial self or soul continuing unchanged. Using the example of cattle and brand, he suggests that the present thought inherits a "title" to the past self, owning it, as it were, by a title that did not lapse. This would be similar to a long succession of cattle owners, each of whom receives the original title of inheritance. So the "title" of a collective self is passed on from one thought to another "in some analogous way." James calls the transmission of title from owner to owner an obvious fact. As one pulse of thought dies away, it is replaced by another. The succeeding thought recognizes the former by the warmth that characterizes it (PP 321–22).

There is one final point to be cleared up, namely, the act of appropriation of one thought by another. James admits that this may be obscure and he attempts to clarify it. To begin with, the present thought must be other than the preceding. A thing can never appropriate itself or disown itself by passing itself on to a successor. There must be an agent that appropriates and disowns, and that is the present thought itself. Firmly situated in the present, it appropriates to itself and it is the hook from which hangs the chain of past selves. James concludes by calling his own description of consciousness a "psychologic fact" needing no other agent. It is sufficient to say that the passing thought is the thinker. In this, personal identity consists (PP 322–24).

Undoubtedly more could be said regarding James's theory of personal identity. The above treatment has been selective, with the choice of details being guided by the intent of making a comparison between Hume and James. The question may now be asked: Which theory seems to be preferable? On the positive side, James makes some important advances over the Humean view. As a psychologist he does not evaluate Hume's treatment of causation. He focuses on the psychology of consciousness, and here he does his best work. In my view, he shows convincingly that Hume misses the most significant aspect of consciousness and personal identity, which is the unity characterizing both. James recognizes that introspective observation uncovers a diversity in consciousness which has not been adequately considered in the past. He gives credit to Hume on this point. But he also maintains that unity is an even more evident datum and has been all but ignored in the Humean account. James undertakes to reconcile both unity and diversity in a manner that not only satisfies feeling but also is consistent with the facts. His description of the experience of shock following silence has become a classic, and his psychological reflection on the persistence of the feeling of self from past to present is creative and persuasive. He has invoked the quality of resemblance found in successive states, but he is quite clear, as Hume was not, that the perceptions resemble one another *as perceptions* in that all share a warmth and intimacy giving rise to the feeling of self and personal identity. In all this, James has not been surpassed in his attempt to provide a corrective for Humean atomism.

But has James succeeded completely in his endeavor? There are good reasons for arguing that he has not. His example of the "herd" is clumsy and forced. It is the weakest section in all of his writings. The metaphors of brand, title, and the passing on of title from owner to owner simply repeat and indeed heighten Hume's atomism. The passing thought that is the thinker turns out to be a perfectly distinct phenomenon, and so is every thought in succession. His explanation of how one thought "appropriates" another is obscure on his own admission, and he does little to clarify it. In fact it is rendered more opaque by his statement that "who owns the last self owns the self before the last, for whatever possesses the possessor possesses the possessed" (PP 332). Finally he fails at one point to break away from atomistic vocabulary, for in describing the Thought or the self as "the hook from which the chain of past selves dangles" (PP 340), he uses the word "chain" which on an earlier occasion he had rejected in favor of "stream" (PP 233).

In the end, James dismisses the alternative of a metaphysical substance or soul to account for the unity of consciousness and personal identity. One reason is the scope of his psychology. As we already noted, James professed to be working out a psychology that was positivistic, non-metaphysical, and verifiable. In the early pages of the *Principles*, he stated that he would take no account of the soul at that time. He acknowledged that his approach would be "only a provisional halting-place" and would require further thought. Meanwhile he grants that the spiritualist may continue to believe in it (PP 191). Later on, after his treatment of consciousness and personal identity, he returns to the question of soul. He finds himself torn between two conflicting convictions of common sense. One moves him to his theory of the passing thought as thinker. But common sense also drives him to admit some Arch-Ego in the form of the soul of scholastic metaphysics or Kant's transcendental Ego, both of which he took to be attempts to satisfy the demand of common sense (PP 321). He finally rejects soul because of difficulties in explaining substantiality, spirituality, immortality, and responsibility before God. He concludes that soul is *"needless for expressing the actual subjective phenomena of consciousness as they appear"* (PP 326). Again he allows the reader the liberty of believing in soul if "he finds any comfort in the idea," but his own reasonings, while not establishing its non-existence, "have only proved its superfluity for scientific purposes" (PP 331–32).

On the question of soul, I think that James has in general adopted a reasonable position in accord with his psychological perspective. But I also think that he can be faulted on two counts. First, he believes that his explanation provides all that is necessary for a coherent theory. I have tried to show that it has serious weaknesses. Further, the overriding reason which persuades him to reject soul is that there are many difficulties that can be raised against it. And these difficulties he does raise. Unfortunately he devotes to them fewer than ten pages out of the thirteen hundred pages his multi-volume work comprises (PP 325–32). This is hardly an adequate treatment of a topic that would have to be more fully and more carefully nuanced. It would have been better if he had remained faithful to his earlier position that soul has no place in a psychological study.

On balance, I would conclude that James presents a theory that is decidedly more faithful to and consistent with experience than that of Hume. But it is still beset with serious gaps. In the end he has not made a convincing case for a continued unified self or for a viable alternative to a substantial soul.

PEIRCE

So far the emphasis has been given to personal identity since this was the emphasis given by Locke, Hume, and James. They were trying to answer the question: Is that which I call "myself" at one moment identical with the self at another moment? In a sense, this is an ontological question in the classical mode, for it involves the position one will adopt on the permanence of a substance continuing essentially the same through time and a variety of activities.

As we have seen, one of the first challenges that Locke and Hume raised was that concerning substance. Both of them called into question our ability to form an idea of substance, and though

Locke did not deny the reality of substance, he laid the ground-work for Hume's eventual rejection of it. Consequently both of them set about to explain personal identity through their empirical epistemology. Locke seemed to suggest, and Hume definitely affirmed, that the self is a series of individual conscious states or perceptions. James was dissatisfied with Hume's position, mainly because it did not adequately explain that which seems over-whelmingly evident through a reflection on our conscious states, namely, that the self is not a series of discrete atomic particles but a continuous stream. Ultimately he put aside the notion of sub-stance, not because he denied it, but because he felt it was not needed from the point of view of psychology. I have already critiqued his attempt and indicated where it was inadequate.

In Peirce, we find a different emphasis. His primary concern is not with personal identity as addressed by the British empiricists but with the human person as a self that fully comes to be, develops, and grows through its openness to things outside itself, especially through its relation to and intercommunication with other selves. This is an aspect of the self which has been fruitfully examined by American pragmatists and process philosophers, among others. As an aside, it should be noted that this concern was not entirely neglected by previous philosophers. One has only to recall that Plato and Aristotle could not conceive of an individual except as a member of the polis and as one fulfilling one's role in a social and political context. The medievalists, too, for all their emphasis on self as a substance remaining essentially the same yet changing in significant ways, thought of the self in relation to other selves and to a social and political community.

The developmental side of a person is, then, eminently worth pursuing for the rich dimensions that it reveals about the self. But for all that, Locke and Hume took a crucial step in undermining the notion of substance. They brought personal identity to the forefront of philosophical debate in a way that was radically different from the Greek, medieval, and Cartesian approaches. Their task was to explain self in terms of an empiricist epistemol-ogy and psychology which were basically atomistic and, to in-dulge in a pun, without substance. Once raised, the question of personal identity has become one that cannot ultimately be avoided, though it is possible for one to think that it can be suppressed. In this section, I shall consider what answer Peirce gave to the problem.

One area of concern for Peirce's critics and for me as well is precise his treatment of the self as substance. Vincent Colapietro, is aware of this concern. His strategy is to show that Peirce "explicitly espoused substance in the old sense (in what he did not hesitate to call the Aristotelian sense) of a thing that endures over time in such a way as to retain its identity, despite undergoing continuous and even profound changes."[3] I would like to examine the texts offered by Colapietro to see if indeed Peirce can be defended as holding substance. The following is cited by Colapietro to show that, though for Peirce atomic particles are the most concrete entities in the physical universe, they are not absolutely discrete in all aspects.

> If an atom had no regular attractions and repulsions, if its mass was at one instant nothing, at another a ton, at another a negative quantity, if its motion instead of being continuous, consisted in a series of leaps from one place to another without passing through any intervening places, and if there were no definite relations between its different positions, velocities and directions of displacement, if it were at one time in one place and at another in a dozen; [then] such a disjointed plurality of phenomena would not make up any existing thing. Not only substance, but events, too, are constituted by their regularities [CP 1.411].

In my view, this text sheds no light on substance; in fact it seems to reject it. The last sentence of the quotation seems to give it all away. Hume himself would simply agree that both substance and events are constituted by their regularities, without being committed to substance as an abiding entity undergoing changes. Actually *events* is an unfortunate term since these too can be construed as discrete happenings, as Hume seems to think. Nor is Peirce any clearer when he calls a thing or a substance "a cluster or habit of reactions" and "a center of forces" (CP 4.157) or "bundles of habits" whereby an individual is a continuity of relations and hence something persistent and permanent (CP 1.414). Hume would have no problem with persistent and continuous behavior; in fact, he insists on it as operative in nature. "Bundles of habits" are ambiguous since we are not told precisely what they are.

Hume, we remember, called the self a bundle or collection of different perceptions which quickly pass by in succession. It is not at all clear how Peirce would differ from Hume on this point.

There is one strand of Peirce's thought which might be pursued if one were to make a case for the reality of substance in Peirce. It is his concept of power in relation to cause and effect. In the previous chapter, I argued that Peirce held for a power or potency in physical objects according to which they act in regular ways. Whether one states that in general fire heats and material objects fall when released or whether one claims that the same particular object acts in regular, predictable ways, Peirce held that this is so because a real potency exists which will be activated under similar conditions. One *could* pursue the matter further and conclude to an abiding substance in which the potency inheres, or, perhaps better, to an abiding entity which can and will act in particular ways given a like set of conditions. I believe that this is where Colapietro, too is leading when he states that "as a continuity of reactions or a regularity of behavior, [an existent thing] reveals in its very reactions or behavior the presence of thirdness."[4] Habits too could be understood in this way. It could then be argued that Peirce *implicitly* holds for the classical notion of substance, and this would open the way for the substantial nature of person. But, so far as I know, Peirce does not explicitly move in that direction. I find this curious, since he exhibits a considerable knowledge of medieval and scholastic philosophy. It is curious, too, that the texts in which he deals with substance tend more to a Humean position.

As a concluding remark, I would emphasize that one must ultimately confront the question: Who or what is it that acts or develops, either at any given moment or over a period of time? Locke, Hume, and James explicitly addressed that question. I have tried to show the weakness of their positions. Peirce, on the other hand, does not clearly endorse substance, and on this point I am a bit surprised and disappointed. However, a theory of substance seems implicit in his development of habits and thirdness.

Dewey

Dewey's early years are frequently called his Hegelian or idealistic period. They extend roughly from his graduate studies at Johns Hopkins, 1882–1884, to about 1891. This designation is understandable; his doctoral dissertation was on "The Psychology of Kant," and he took courses with George Sylvester Morris whose Neo-Hegelian philosophical viewpoint greatly influenced him. Mention should also be made of Dewey's acquaintance with the "new psychology" or physiological psychology through courses offered by G. Stanley Hall, newly appointed to the Chair of Psychology at Johns Hopkins in 1882.

What is less often mentioned, however, is that Morris also taught seminars in the history of philosophy. In a letter to H. A. P. Torrey, his former professor at the University of Vermont, Dewey relates that in one of Morris' courses he read Aristotle's *De anima* or "The Treatise on the Soul."[5] As we shall see, Dewey's Hegelian years can also be called his Aristotelian period. This will be illustrated in his early view of the self as shown in two of his writings published in 1886, an article "Soul and Body" and his first book, *Psychology*. The former definitely manifests the influence of Aristotle on his theory of the self, while the latter work is less clearly Aristotelian and may be called Hegelian or idealistic. The purpose of this discussion will be to show that, unlike Peirce and James, Dewey early on had a theory of self as an abiding, permanent substance, a position he was to abandon after the 1890s.

In his paper, Dewey's purpose is to explain the relation between soul and body. He also proposes to work out a "physiological psychology" along philosophical lines. Thus he describes the difference between the physical or physiological and the psychological or mental aspects of human activities as well as the relationship between them. His starting point is reflex action or the reaction of the nervous system to some stimulus. Basically a nervous activity is an adjustment of the organism to a change in outward conditions. But the reaction is not random or haphazard; it is directed. As such it is not merely psychical; that is, the psychical is immanent in the physical in the sense that it directs the physical activity to an end. In the pursuit of the end, the psychical selects, responds to, inhibits, controls, and coordinates the various activities. In other words, even in the simplest form of a nervous reaction there are categories and principles which transcend physical causality and which include the category of teleology. This involves not only physical causation but also final and psychical. Dewey proposes an objection to his own position which might be raised by a materialist, namely, that through a long series of accidental happenings, an activity favorable to the organism may take root and give a mere appearance of purpose. This process, it is said, can be explained through the mechanisms of biological evolution, such as variation, selection, survival of the fittest, or heredity. Dewey calls this attempt at explanation "suicidal." It assumes that purpose can arise from accident, that a special case can be elevated to a general law. In short, "the psychical is teleologically immanent in the physical." Though various nerve organs may have their own part to play, they are all coordinated toward the development of the whole. Such coordination is not limited to nervous reactions but includes other activities, such as sensation and higher mental processes. The body is not only a physiological but also a psychophysiological organism (EW 1:98–106).

Dewey then moves to a discussion of soul and its relation to the body. His analysis leads him to conclude that there is "something else" beyond the principle of physical causation, and he calls it the principle of self-developing activity, traditionally known as the soul. In expressing the relation between soul and body, he states that "not only is the soul immanent in the body, as teleological, and subordinating and adjusting its various activities to an end, but the body is the stimulus to the soul." This applies to sensation and to all higher psychical activities of the organism, but it transforms them to something beyond what they are on the physiological level. The soul is *immanent* in the body, it constitutes the latter's unity and end, it transcends it and transforms its activities (EW 1:106–107). With explicit reference to Aristotle, Dewey calls the body the organ of the soul, though he adds that the term *organ* indicates a relationship that is closer than is usually understood because, through the body, the soul reaches the fulfillment of its own nature (EW 1:112). Furthermore, and again in Aristotelian terms, Dewey maintains that the body is constituted as such and continues to develop because of the informing, creative activity of the soul. Finally, "it was the 'master of those who know' that said that the soul was the perfect realization or expression of a natural body, and at the same time, not the product of body, but its very life, its essence, its truth and reality—at once its final and efficient cause (Aristotle, *De Anima*, ii, 1)" (EW 1:114). The pages of "Soul and Body" are remarkable, for they seem to be written by an Aristotelian who was trying to apply the Greek philosopher's theory of soul to the new movement in contemporary physiological psychology. In reading them, one has to keep recalling that they were written by Dewey.

The purpose of Dewey's *Psychology* is expressed in the Preface to the book. His basic standpoint is that of a philosopher who is examining another discipline to see how it impacts upon philosophy. This approach was not unique to Dewey. Without going back further than the post-medieval period, we may note that Descartes attempted to incorporate mathematics into his philosophical framework, Locke was influenced by Boyle's corpuscular theory, and Hume by Newtonian physics. As we have seen, Dewey was impressed by the new psychology and particularly physiological psychology. After all, these had only recently emerged with Wilhelm Wundt's *Grundzuge der physiologischen Psychologie* in 1873–1874. In 1879 Wundt founded at Leipzig the first formal psychological laboratory. Hall, Dewey's teacher at Johns Hopkins, had studied for two years with Wundt and was the latter's first American student.[6]

In a sense Dewey's situation was somewhat different from that of Descartes, Locke, and Hume. They were confronting scientific ideas which had already begun to be distinguished from philosophy in terms of the questions raised and the method by which these questions were addressed. This was not quite the case with psychology. As far back as Aristotle, the very etymology of the word meant the study of the soul and mental states and included the relation of soul and body, the spiritual and material. From his own philosophical background—Hegelian, idealistic, Aristotelian, or a combination of these—Dewey was aware that these philosophical traditions were facing something quite new but not fully separate from philosophy. And so, at the beginning of his Preface to *Psychology*, he stated that any textbook on psychology for classroom use had to address the question: "What shall be its attitude toward philosophic principles?" It is one that simply could not be avoided. When psychology was a composite of logic, ethics, and metaphysics, the question did not arise. Psychology constituted a good introduction into philosophy, and the writer of a textbook stood on familiar ground. But this was no longer the case, for recently psychology seemed to warrant a treatment in its own right (EW 2:3).

The latter route, however, was not the one that Dewey chose to follow. He still felt that there were philosophical questions which could not be avoided, since they were imbedded within psychology itself—for example, the nature of the mind and its relation to reality. Another reason for his choice was that traditionally psychology had been the path by which college students embarked upon the study of philosophy. Dewey elected, therefore, to accomplish both tasks, that is, to preserve the role of psychology as an introduction to philosophy and at the same time to incorporate the investigations of recent experts in the new psychology. He recognized the difficulty of the enterprise, but he felt it was the best route for him to take at that time. In the following, the focus will be on what he has to say about the self.

At the very beginning of his text, Dewey defines psychology as the science of the facts or phenomena of the self. He tries to explain what he means by self through other terms: ego, or the fact that self can recognize itself as I, as a distinct existence or personality; mind, or the self as intelligent; soul, or self as distinct from body yet connected with it; psychical, which serves to distinguish data of the self from physical phenomena; subject, indicating that self "lies under" and unites feelings, purposes, and ideas and distinguishes self from objects; spirit, referring to the higher activities of self which are different from material objects and mechanical activities. The basic fact of self is consciousness, by which it not only is but knows that it is. It exists for itself and is different from a stone that exists but is not aware of it; a stone does not exist for itself but only for some consciousness. It follows from this that the self is directly conscious of its own psychological states, which are known only by the self. The self may be communicated to others by facial appearance or sounds, but it cannot be known by others directly. The fact that a self or consciousness exists is a unique individual fact (EW 2:7–9). Though the self goes through many conscious states and changes, it remains the same amid these changes. It is the role of memory to identify self as permanent amid its changing experiences. Through memory, the mind unites these experiences, distinguishes past experiences from present ones, and also discerns their difference from the present permanent self. This distinction between a then and a now, a past and a present, would not be possible without an awareness of the same self as present then and now (EW 2:165).

In sum, then, for Dewey the self or soul or mind is a permanent being intimately related to a body but superior to it and transcending and transforming bodily activities; the soul abides under changing mental states and gives the individual its stability and continuity. His position follows closely the classical meaning of substance as begun by Aristotle whom Dewey mentions by name in his paper "Soul and Body."

Such was Dewey's position regarding the self during his Hegelian, idealistic, Aristotelian period. It was not to last very long. Dewey's uneasiness about the difficulty of the project envisioned in his *Psychology* was not without good reason. Herbert Schneider relates that by the 1891 third revised edition, Dewey shifted from idealism to the "new psychology." In Schneider's view, Dewey was trying to put new wine into old bottles, "an imprudent practice" (EW 2:xxiv). The reasons for the shift in Dewey's thinking would require a long and detailed treatment and they are no doubt familiar enough. The following points, however, are worth mentioning.

William James's *Principles of Psychology* appeared in 1890, and Dewey on several occasions acknowledged his debt to it. For example, in his 1925 paper "The Development of American Pragmatism," Dewey states that James led him to the view that coordinated responses in humans, though still called teleological, have their origin in biological adaptive behavior which makes intelligent projections regarding ways of adapting to environmental conditions (LW 2:15–16). The influence of this aspect of James's *Principles* can be seen in Dewey's 1896 paper "The Reflex Arc Concept in Psychology." Dewey returned to the description of the reflex which he had discussed in "Soul and Body." In the latter paper, he had emphasized the unity, coordination, and teleology of the stimulus–response sequence, but he attributed these ultimately to something transcending physical activities, namely, the soul. A decade later he repeated his criticism of the view of the reflex which explained it as a series of three disjointed and com-

plete parts—sensory stimulus, central activity, and motor dis-
charge. Rather, these should be viewed as divisions of labor
coordinated and unified into a single whole. The response is not
a totally new experience—for example, the burning sensation in
the hand of a child as distinct from the sensation of the light of a
candle, and the intervening movement toward the light. The
sequence is not an arc or a series of jerks, but a circuit, a reconsti-
tution of a continued experience (EW 5:98–99). In his explanation,
Dewey retains the concept of coordination and unity of the experience adapted to an end, whether that end be the continuation of
the species, preserving life, or simple movement to a place (EW
5:104). But now he rejects "an extra-experimental soul" and aban-
dons talk of the psychological as transcending the physical or
material (EW 5:99). Reflex responses as well as conscious states in
general are explained by basic biological capacities to react in
various ways to meet specific changes in the environment. In this
article Dewey was already moving toward the biological model
of interaction or transaction between organism and environment
which became central to this theory of experience.

It is perhaps in *Experience and Nature* (1925) that Dewey gave
his most detailed and complete theory of the self. By then he had
long moved away from his Aristotelian, idealistic stage, though
on his own admission some aspects of Hegel's philosophy had a
lasting influence on his thought. But regarding the self, he had
departed from any semblance of a substance that abides through
changing activities. What characterizes all living things is organization which enables them to marshal their energies in completing
the need–demand–satisfaction sequence. Living things are "psychophysical," or a step above mere physical beings. But that term
does not denote a separation or hierarchy of being, one psychic
and the other physical; nor is there a problem of the relation
between the two. It simply indicates that a living being possesses
certain capabilities and activities not found in inanimate objects
(LW 1:195–96). A human being is characterized by "mind" which
emerges when a body by reason of its more complex and special-
ized organization performs more varied activities to meet compli-
cated situations. These consist more specifically in utilizing the
meaning of past and present experiences and applying them for
the intelligent direction of the future, especially through lan-

guage. It is through language that the activities called psycho-physical become mental, since communication modifies organic ways of acting so that the latter achieve new qualities (LW 1:198, 219, 222).

By now, Dewey had adopted the description of experience as an interaction between an organic self and the environment. In addition, his theory of experience rejects any division between act and outside material, subject and object; both are contained "in an unanalyzed totality." In this description he was setting aside both empirical and idealist divisions which conceived of experience as states of subjective private consciousness separate from nature (LW 1:18–19). But Dewey himself realized that the inevitable question would arise: "Whose experience are we talking about?" The question indicates an objection of one who would argue that experience must exist somewhere and cannot reside vaguely be-tween subject and object. Dewey tries to work out a delicate balance between retaining his original, strong position of interac-tion and a recognition that consciousness is somehow related to a self. He views the question as implying that one must return to the notion that experience is "owned" by someone and conse-quently that it is private and exclusive. He proceeds first to check the move, calling it absurd. To establish this, he uses the example of a house that is owned; it is mine or yours or someone else's. But the attribution of ownership should not obscure its other proper-ties which it has independent of ownership, for example, that it is made of stone or wood, has so many rooms, and so forth. Own-ership does add new relationships: the house is now taxable, outsiders can be excluded from entering it, the owner assumes certain responsibilities and obligations. So it is with experience; it has traits which can be described without reference to self or owner. For that reason it is more proper to say that "it" experiences or is experienced, "it" thinks or is thought, than to say I experience or I think. The experience as it moves along has its own properties and relationships. Where, then, is the self found? Not outside or beneath these relationships but within them. The self is but one of the qualities which make up experience, just as brick and mortar make a house. Of course, as with the house, experience can be considered as owned, and this entails further liabilities as well as enjoyments. But Dewey quickly adds that the self is not the source of the thoughts or its exclusive location. It is rather "a centered organization of energies" (LW 1:178–80).

It is evident that Dewey has departed from the theory of self in its classical mode as some permanent substance. But at the same time he does not wish to revert to an empirical atomism or to an idealistic subjectivism. Likewise, he is rejecting an ontological distinction between soul and body or psychological and physical in its classical sense. Nonetheless human beings are more than physical objects, and the difference consists in the type of organization which enables the human organism to interact with the outside world in ways that are vastly different from those of inanimate objects or living organisms other than humans. Yet self is a concept that is very difficult to ignore, so he attempts to integrate it into his primary meaning of experience as an interaction between organism and the outside world. The self is not independent of experience, "an all-embracing maw" swallowing up all independent properties and relationships into some ego. The fact of ownership is one among other properties, though it is also an additive element introducing new relationships, as in the case of the ownership of a house (LW 1:179).

Finally Dewey recognized the fact that certain terms are still applied to human beings. Two of these are *soul* and *spirit*. He refers to them, but he gives them meanings far different from those he once accepted. For him, soul indicates the characteristics of psychophysical activities insofar as they are organized and unified. A human being is capable of higher activities, such as producing works of art, music, poetry, architecture. Soul is called spirit when the soul or organization is free, developing, not terminal or static. By reason of spirit a human being is quickened in a way that animals are not. "Soul is form, spirit informs. It is the moving function of that of which soul is the substance." These vague terms are faintly reminiscent of his Aristotelian period. But he immediately adds that perhaps the terms soul and spirit ought to be dropped, since they are freighted with "traditional mythology and sophisticated doctrine" (LW 1: 222–24).

In the previous discussion, the texts used from *Experience and Nature* are taken from the later chapters of the book where Dewey was focusing on consciousness, body, and mind. These texts were given priority in order to highlight his position on self. What emerged was a vague picture of self, almost lost or at least submerged in the various details that experience constitutes. But a different picture emerges in earlier sections. There he criticized previous philosophical theories for submerging individuality, whether in primitive tribal cultures, in metaphysical doctrines of fixed categories and organized wholes, or in structured institutions and collective traditions. Though he specifically mentions Greek philosophy and civilization, it is clear from his other writings that he would include the course of history roughly prior to the sixteenth century. But the modern world has witnessed "an extraordinary revolution." The individual was now no longer viewed as complete, fixed, finished but as moving, changing, creative. Individual mind came to be valued as a particular center of initiative, change, desire, thinking, hope (LW 1:162–68). Imagination plays the role of dissolving old objects and forming new ones; mind itself in a unique way mediates between the old and the new by planning and reconstructing of the existing order. This stage of thought and aspiration is an intermediate one situated between the old order of things that has been and the new order which is to be restructured according to imaginative projections and overt action. What is significant here are the characteristics which Dewey attributes to this aspect of mind. On the one hand, he warns against a return to subjectivism or to a transcendental ego (which he calls "a plague"!). He also asserts that this intermediate stage must become social in the further planning and testing of overt action. Nonetheless he insists that the mind or self which he is describing is intrinsically private and incommunicable, fluid and in process of being formed. It is also individual, constructive, and re-creative (LW 1:170–76).

The description that Dewey gives of self in *Experience and Nature* manifests a marked ambivalence. The earlier section stressed individuality and uniqueness, where self is a center of spontaneity and creativity in reacting to old ways of thinking and acting. But when he focuses more sharply on the narrower question of the meaning of self, the latter fades almost into insignificance. How can this paradox be explained? My own feeling is that he tried to reconcile what he took to be two broad currents of thought. The first denigrated individuality, with the result that the self was absorbed into a static state unable to break out of conformity and uniformity. In his view, that outlook did not do justice to the inner spontaneity and creativity of the human person. But he was equally opposed to the view of self as a permanent entity that endured through change; this leads to fixity, subjectivism, and isolation which were primary examples of the splits that he felt were characteristics of previous philosophic viewpoints. The question remains whether his narrower conception of self was able to fulfill the promise of a new and creative self which, in his own words, constituted a revolutionary outlook of the person in modern philosophy.

NOTES

1. Barry Stroud, *Hume* (Boston: Routledge & Kegan Paul, 1977), p. 126.

2. My discussion of James's theory of personal identity is restricted to the *Principles*, Volume I. That volume contains his fullest treatment of it, and there he explicitly confronts Hume. Some commentators claim that James's later works amplify his theory of person, namely, *A Pluralistic Universe* and *Essays in Radical Empiricism*. From my own reading of these works, I would agree that in them he develops the richer dimensions of experience. For this reason, I would add the last two chapters of *Pragmatism* to the above-mentioned works and I shall draw upon these in later chapters. But I do not think that James significantly improves on his notion of personal identity as given in the *Principles*. For example, some feel that his later theory of "pure experience" as developed in Chapter I of *Essays in Radical Empiricism* ought to be considered. But that doctrine is exceedingly difficult to interpret, is highly controversial, and only makes his theory of self more obscure. For a defense of the use of the later works, see Eugene Fontinell, *Self, God, and Immortality: A Jamesian Investigation* (Philadelphia: Temple University Press, 1986), chap. 3–5.

3. Vincent Michael Colapietro, *Peirce's Approach to the Self: A Semiotic Perspective on Human Subjectivity* (New York: State University of New York Press, 1989), pp. 86–87. In this section, I shall criticize Colapietro's book, though in Chapter 5 I shall draw upon it in interpreting Peirce. Hence, though I offer some "friendly amendments" to his position here, I consider his volume to be among the best to appear on Peirce.

4. Ibid., p. 82.

5. See George Dykhuizen, *The Life and Mind of John Dewey* (Carbondale: Southern Illinois University Press, 1973), p. 32.

6. See Edwin G. Boring, *A History of Experimental Psychology* (New York: Appleton-Century-Crofts, 1950), p. 518.

4

MORAL, SOCIAL, AND POLITICAL THEORIES: THE EMPIRICISTS

THE PREVIOUS CHAPTER FOCUSED on the narrow problem of personal identity. Consideration of further dimensions of the person was carefully excluded, not because these are unimportant but because personal identity was thought to be a prior question that had to be addressed. It is now time to take up the moral, social, and political theories of our five philosophers and to trace and compare what they had to say about them. It was my original intention to devote a separate chapter to each of these topics. But it soon became clear that in Locke, Hume, and Dewey, these three themes are closely related and should be taken together. On the other hand, neither Peirce nor James developed a full-blown position in all three areas. For all that, it seemed best to preserve the format of the preceding chapters and to take each philosopher in turn. Since a single chapter would be unduly long, the discussion has been divided into two chapters, one for the empiricists and one for the pragmatists.

LOCKE

It is customary to highlight two aspects of Locke's moral theory. The first is that things are good or evil in relation to pleasure or pain. This leads some to conclude that self-interest and even hedonism are at the basis of this moral theory. The second aspect is that morality is capable of demonstration. My own agenda will be to clarify precisely what Locke means by pleasure and pain, good and evil and thus to examine whether these in fact have a utilitarian or hedonistic flavor. Regarding the statement that ethics can be demonstrated, the best that one can do is to point out the ambiguities in Locke's position and to expose its weaknesses.

An appropriate place to begin is the oft-quoted text of Locke: "Things then are Good or Evil, only in reference to Pleasure or Pain" (EU 229). This statement is made in the context of his enumeration of ideas in Book II of the *Essay*, and my present topic is taken up in Chapter XX, "Modes of Pleasure and Pain." We recall that Locke, and Hume too, drew up a catalogue of ideas as mental phenomena known through reflection on internal experience. Pleasure or pain, delight or uneasiness, are simple ideas which generally accompany a sensation originating from the outside or a perception originating in the mind. Good and evil are the names given to whatever produces these experiences. A good causes or increases pleasure, lessens pain, preserves other goods or prevents evil. An evil is that which causes or increases pain, lessens pleasure, or prevents us from obtaining some good. Locke states that the origin of pleasure and pain can be assigned either to body or mind, but ultimately they are both affections of the mind. I would take his meaning to be that they are conscious states. Another term that can be used is *passion*.

Now, it should be noted that, at this stage, Locke is not talking about *moral* good or evil. He is using these terms in a morally neutral sense to describe the various affective states or passions that we experience. We do sort out two different kinds of objects, those which please and those which displease. So far he is merely cataloguing these affections and objects without making a judgment about their moral quality. In addition, the pleasures and pains which he is considering are not limited to what are usually called sensual. They can include "not only bodily Pain and Pleasure, but whatever *Delight* or *Uneasiness* is felt by us, whether arising from any grateful, or unacceptable Sensation or Reflection" (EU 232). Thus love or hate, joy or sorrow can arise from the taste of grapes as well as from relations with children or friends. The same applies to hope, fear, and despair, or anger and envy.

Locke concedes that many other examples could be given, such as the pleasure of eating and drinking, musing and rational conversation, the search and discovery of truth, and contrariwise the pain of hunger and thirst, or foolish disagreements with others, and many more. But he is satisfied that the examples he has given are sufficient to explain his meaning.

Locke immediately relates pleasure and pain to the notion of power. In a long and wide-ranging discussion of 55 pages and 73 paragraphs, he covers active and passive powers of the mind, freedom, and good and evil.[1] His treatment of good and evil leads into moral considerations involving God, a future life, and natural law. The longest section has to do with the will and is in effect a psychological study of the motivating influences on free choice. His basic question is "What is it that determines the will in regard to our actions?" (EU 250). The main force is uneasiness or pain in the absence of some good. If one is content with one's present state, or, in other words, when there is no uneasiness, no action will follow. It may even be the case that a person feeling the pinch of poverty or living a debauched life realizes that material goods are attainable or that virtue is necessary for a good human existence both here and hereafter. Yet the person will not be moved to action as long as there is no desire to improve the situation. But once there is the realization that the present condition of uneasiness or pain is preventing the attainment of pleasure, that is, happiness, desire will be aroused and the first necessary step will be taken to remove the cause of pain and to make use of those things that produce happiness. But the step will not be taken if reflection remains on the theoretical level. Experience shows that there are some who fully understand the ineffable, infinite, and eternal joys of heaven. Yet they make no effort toward possessing such absent goods because their wills are not aflame with desire for them. Instead their attention is riveted on their present uneasiness, which they seek to remove by some present worldly good. They do not see that virtue and its rewards are a part of their complete happiness (EU 255–62).

Locke further maintains that the studious and persistent pursuit of true and solid happiness comprises the highest perfection of our intellectual nature and our greatest good. Consequently we must be on our guard lest we mistake false for genuine happiness.

This requires careful consideration and evaluation of particular goods to see if they are in accord with our true end. Human beings have the great privilege of being able to weigh particular goods and to make proper choices; more than that, they have an obligation to do so. Unfortunately, not all agree regarding what constitutes true happiness. People desire a variety of objects: study, knowledge, hawking and hunting, luxury and debauchery, riches, food and drink. The main reason for this is their belief that this life is final with no hope of life beyond the grave. At the same time, those who make wrong judgments about good and evil are responsible to themselves for the bad consequences of their actions. Human liberty does not allow one to violate with impunity "the eternal Law and Nature of things." What is needed is a change of one's perspective. A person must see the necessity of virtue and religion for happiness and be aware of the delight or misery of a future life and the reality of God as judge rendering to each according to one's good or evil deeds. Choices will then be made, not according to transient pleasure or pain but in view of eternal happiness hereafter (EU 266–74). Morality will be established on its true foundation, and everyone who goes contrary to these norms is not acting as a rational creature and is to blame for not making proper use of human understanding (EU 281–82).

It is illuminating to review the development of Locke's thought. At first he simply analyzes pleasure and pain as belonging to his long list of ideas, without introducing moral considerations. The analysis is continued in the context of identifying the factors that motivate the will to action. Pleasure and pain, happiness and misery, good and evil are central notions. But almost imperceptibly he begins to make judgments regarding the nature of the happiness that one ought to pursue. Such happiness is not limited to sensible or sensual pleasures or pains. It gradually becomes apparent that his norms are the proper end of human understanding and human life, especially as these are or ought to be directed to a future life of happiness established by God. It seems that Locke is not a hedonist in the usual meaning of the term. He relates morality, virtue, and vice to one's true final end here and hereafter. All this is recognizable as constituting a natural law theory of morality, even though it is not explicitly developed.

If in the *Essay* Locke had gone no further in his discussion of virtue, vice, and morality, he could be viewed as presenting a position within the natural law tradition. But a bit later in the *Essay* he returns to the question, this time under the heading "Of Other Relations" (EU 348ff.). He is still developing the various ideas of the mind, and among complex ideas are relations formed by comparing ideas. This leads him to moral relations each of which is "the Conformity, or Disagreement, Men's voluntary Actions have to a Rule, to which they are referred, and by which they are judged of" (EU 350). The voluntary actions in reference to a rule are now explicitly called moral actions. Locke makes mention of his previous discussion of good and evil as being things which produce pleasure or pain. "*Morally Good and Evil*, then, is only the Conformity or Disagreement of our voluntary Actions to some Law, whereby Good or Evil is drawn on us, from the Will and Power of the Law-Maker; which Good and Evil, Pleasure or Pain, attending our observance, or breach of the Law, by the Decree of the Law-Maker, is what we call *Reward* and *Punishment*" (EU 351). Locke has now brought together the elements which he claims must be considered in any discussion of morality: namely, human action according to a rule imposed by a lawgiver, with sanctions for the observance or violation of the law.

Locke then enumerates three kinds of laws: (1) the divine law, promulgated by God either through the light of nature or the voice of revelation and dealing with actions called morally good and evil, or duties and sins; (2) civil law, the rule set by the Commonwealth, which judges actions to be criminal or not; (3) the law of opinion or reputation or fashion, having to do with virtue, the norm being reputation and discredit, praise and blame (EU 352). Locke maintains that the divine law promulgated by God is so evident that no one could be so "brutish" as to deny it. Since we are God's creatures, he has the right to direct our actions to what is best, and he also has the power to enforce his law by future rewards and punishments. This law is the only real basis for moral good and evil. Civil law is imposed by the Commonwealth, fulfilling its duty to protect the lives, liberties, and possessions of its citizens and having the power to guarantee compliance with the law by appropriate sanctions. So far, there does not seem to be any grounds for misunderstanding or criticizing what Locke is saying.

But it is the third law, that of opinion or reputation, that gives rise to ambiguities, and it is often taken to be Locke's final position. According to Locke, actions are considered to be virtue or vice according to whether they are praised or blamed, approved or disapproved, by the general opinion or fashion current in a society at a given time and place. It may be the case that the general opinion differs according to "the different temper, Education, Fashion, Maxims or Interest" of different societies. What is considered virtue in one place may be vice in another, but the norm is the same, namely, the public approval or disapproval that prevails. Locke even asserts that this norm will be evident to anyone who considers the question. Furthermore, claims Locke, anyone familiar with human nature and history will realize that commendation and disgrace, in short, the law of opinion or fashion, is the one that exerts the most powerful influence on human behavior. Most people govern themselves mainly, if not only, by this law, and regard lightly the law of God or the Commonwealth. If they do reflect on the punishments for breaking God's law, they think they can amend their ways by repenting and making their peace with God, or they believe they can disobey civil laws without being caught. But there are few who can endure the dislike, condemnation, contempt, and disgrace that follow upon actions that go against the general opinion of those with whom they associate, whether these be friends, members of a club, or fellow citizens (EU 356–57).

It is Locke's rendition of the third law which evokes the criticism that, in the last analysis, he gave priority to public opinion as the rule for moral behavior. In my view, this is a misreading of his position and fails to consider some important aspects of his thought. For one thing, he makes it quite clear that the divine law is the most important one of his moral theory. In Book I of the *Essay*, he had argued against innate ideas. The focal point of this attack was not primarily Descartes but the exaggerations of contemporary English divines who claimed that moral and religious principles were innate.[2] At the same time, he criticized the opposite extreme of those who denied that there is a divine law knowable by human reason independent of positive revelation (EU 75). In his discussion of the first of the three moral laws, the divine law, he again held that it could be known by reason or revelation.

In answer to an objection regarding the law of opinion or fashion, he makes it clear that he is enumerating the rules that humans in fact follow and not making a judgment at that point as to whether they are true or false. He does claim that a proper reading of human nature and of history will show that the third rule is the most powerful in practice. However, he adds that a full reading of chapters from Books I and II of the *Essay* would make evident his position regarding the priority of the eternal and unchangeable nature of right and wrong, virtue and vice (EU 354). My own reading of Locke, then, leads me to conclude that he gave priority to an unalterable divine moral law known through revelation or reason. Also there is no doubt about his conviction that the third law was the one he considered *in fact* to be the one most commonly followed and the most effective in motivating people to action.

Yet it is one thing for Locke to claim that he is developing a natural law theory of morality and quite another for him to justify that claim. In the texts examined so far, he has included the main elements of a classical, or at least medieval, natural moral law: Human beings by nature are directed to the final end of happiness with God; they are under a law promulgated by God, known either by divine revelation or by reason, obliging them to seek that happiness; and they will be rewarded or punished hereafter according to their actions. But none of these elements is sustained in terms of his own philosophy. His proof for God's existence begins with the assumption of an intuitive knowledge of the principle of causality and proceeds in demonstrative fashion through God's various attributes (EU 619ff.). But nowhere does he indicate how such a line of argument can be justified by his empirical epistemology or, even if such a procedure were valid regarding finite reality, how it could be applied to a transcendent, infinite being. He also held that reason cannot prove the spirituality and immortality of the soul. Effectively, then, his natural law morality was left without sufficient grounding in his own empirical philosophy.

Another puzzling aspect of Locke's moral theory is his attempt to show that morality is capable of demonstration. It is clear, to me at least, that he wanted to put morality on as firm a foundation as possible, and so he gave priority to a natural law coming from God. But he also intended to integrate morality into his epistemology. He tries, then, to justify the certainty of ethics in terms of his theory of ideas. One type of knowledge which attains certainty is demonstration. The mind perceives the agreement or disagreement of ideas by comparing them (EU 532). It goes beyond the ideas and perceives their relation. In this comparison, Locke claims that the mind does not need to attend to the particular aspects of the ideas compared. For example, in viewing Cajus, a man, as a father, one does not consider the particular aspects of this particular individual but only Cajus as man, and the same with father. Other relations are father and son, husband and wife (EU 319–20). The mind does not have to face the problem of real versus nominal essences that arises if actual things in reality are considered. Demonstration, therefore, deals with real essences (EU 517, 643). Against this background, Locke thinks that he is justified in saying that moral knowledge is as certain as mathematics. Both involve the agreement or disagreement of ideas; the ideas themselves do not deal with actual existences whose nominal essences alone can be known, but with archetypes or real essences. Just as mathematics abstracts from real figures, so moral discourse abstracts from the lives of real people and from the actual existence of virtue or vice (EU 365–66). Locke does claim, however, that moral propositions can apply to actual situations. If it be true in theory, for example, that murder deserves the punishment of death, it will also be true of any action that fulfills the meaning of murder.

There are obvious problems here. If the proposition "murder deserves death" were admitted to be valid, the direct application to a real situation could easily be made. But the identity between murder and capital punishment is not at all obvious. One could ask what murder means and how its meaning is derived; furthermore no rational arguments are given to sustain the judgment that capital punishment is an appropriate sanction. Locke succeeds no better in other examples that he proposes: where there is no property, there is no injustice, and no government allows absolute liberty (EU 549–50). He as much as admits that these propositions are tautologies for, regarding the first, he states that the idea of property is a right to anything, while injustice is the negation of that right; as for the second, he claims that the idea of government is the formation of laws demanding obedience, while the idea of absolute liberty would allow one to do anything, including the violation of the laws. In effect, Locke's attempt to defend the demonstrative character of morality involves either unjustified claims or tautologies. It is plausible to assume that such obvious weaknesses can be explained by his eagerness to give philosophical grounding for the God-given unchangeable nature of morality that is the center of his moral theory.

It can be seen, then, that Locke's moral theory as developed in the *Essay* is brief, sketchy, and at times philosophically inconsistent. It is also highly speculative, without engaging in particular moral issues. But there is one more aspect that should be noted. Little is said about the close relationship of individual moral agents to their fellow human beings. In some sense, civil law and the law of fashion have social implications, since a reference to others constitutes the individual as a moral person. But that reference is subordinate to what Locke takes to be the essential element of moral good and evil, namely, conformity or disagreement of voluntary actions to a law. Other human beings are merely points of reference specifying those to whom moral actions are directed by a law. Moreover, the force motivating action according to a rule is not the good that will accrue to others but the reward or punishment that will result for the agent. This is true also regarding the divine law where little is said of abiding by the law out of love for the supreme lawgiver and where again the emphasis is on reward or punishment.

Locke's moral theory, then, is intensely inner-directed, and the individual's behavior toward others is conditioned by its effect upon one's own self. For this reason, the charge that his moral theory is basically one of self-interest is entirely justified. Further evidence of this is his feeble attempt to show that "in great measure" the law of fashion coincides with the divine law. For people generally, if they have any sense or reason, see that it is in their self-interest not to act in ways that cause confusion and mischief in society but to preserve the good order of things. And since conformity either to the divine law or to the law of fashion achieves that goal, Locke is confident that the law of nature is "pretty well preserved" (EU 356). But in arguing his case, he has also made self-interest the common element of the two laws.

The question could be asked: Philosophically, what is the origin of Locke's individualistic view of the moral self? If only the *Essay* is considered, I suppose one could argue that it is another manifestation of the atomism that runs through a good part of the *Essay*. It begins with his treatment of ideas, which are described as isolated conscious states called simple ideas and which are combined to form complex ones. Personal identity consists essentially in the consciousness of acts of thinking. As I insisted in the previous chapter, a philosopher in developing a theory of person is forced to some theory of self-identity, but I also indicated that there should be more to it than that. In other words, a social context or outgoing relationships with others should be developed. This social context Locke does not provide. Consequently it is plausible to conclude from the *Essay* that Locke's atomism in his theory of ideas led quite naturally into his individualistic view of the moral person.

If one were to attend only to the number of times that Locke mentions natural law or the law of nature in his political writings, it would be easy to conclude that there is a close connection between his moral and political theories. This is the opportune time to test that hypothesis and to see if it can bear careful scrutiny. It will not be my purpose to engage in a long discussion of all the complex issues contained in his works on government or to trace the role he played in the emergence of political liberalism. I shall concentrate only on his *Second Treatise of Government* published in 1690, the same year in which the *Essay* appeared.[3] Selection of details is made with our philosophers in mind, especially Hume and Dewey. Some final comments will then be offered.

In 1666, Locke made the acquaintance of Anthony Ashley Cooper, later first Earl of Shaftesbury, who became a prominent figure in English politics. Their close friendship had a lasting influence on Locke's interest in political affairs.[4] These affairs in turn were closely related to the religious conflicts that had in large part been responsible for the Civil War in England in 1642 during Locke's early life, resulting in the beheading of Charles I in 1649, and later were to lead to the "Glorious Revolution" ending with the deposition of James II in 1689 and the ascent of the Hanoverian, William III, to the throne. In 1689 the Toleration Act was passed, formally allowing religious freedom. Though certain groups were not tolerated, for example, Roman Catholics, atheists, and others, the

Act did given legal recognition to liberty of worship which went far beyond what most of Europe had permitted. At the same time, it weakened the power that the Church of England had exercised in religious and political matters.[5] In view of these events, Locke's intellectual career has been portrayed as an attempt to formulate a so-called "civil theology" which would provide a sense of shared purpose and stability for a realm that had been torn apart by religious conflicts. Locke's agenda operated on two fronts: First he argued that, because of the hostility among the various Christian sects, religion could no longer guarantee unity and stability; and second he tried to delineate some objective and certain criteria according to which government could be shaped and citizens could act. His program would then mark out principles that all citizens could accept and that would enable them to live in peace and harmony. In effect, Locke was proposing a political theory to replace the Christian religion as a stabilizing influence in the realm.[6]

There is no doubt that natural law or the law of nature or of reason is the bedrock upon which Locke builds his political theory in the *Second Treatise*. The starting point is the "state of nature" or of society prior to the formation of civil society. Despite his occasional references to concrete cases of such societies (T2 §§14–15), it is not entirely clear that he believed the state of nature to be historically factual. Perhaps it was only "a rational concept and *analytical* unit" introduced as a device for laying the groundwork for his theory of natural law and political society, as James Collins seems to suggest.[7] But he is clear as to what basic rights belong to human beings independent of civil society. In the state of nature, all have equal freedom to act and to "dispose of their possessions, and Persons" as they wish without subordination to anyone else, provided they adhere to the law of nature (T2 §4). This law is known by reason, and it obliges all so that, though they are equal and independent, they may not encroach upon the "Life, Health, Liberty, or Possessions" of others (T2 §6). Ultimately this law has God for its author, for he is our maker and owner; proximately the law is founded on our common human nature. By the same law; all have the right to punish those who violate the law; otherwise it would be meaningless and ineffective (T2 §7).

Again, it is the law of nature given by God that drives people

to form societies "under strong obligations of Necessity, Convenience, and Inclination" (T2 §77). Civil government is formed so
that each one's property (life, liberty, and estate) may be protected, violations of the law punished, and appropriate penalties
applied. All members, therefore, surrender their natural power
and private judgment into the hands of the political community.
In this consists the origin of the legislative and executive powers
of civil society (T2 §§87–88). But, as is well known, there is another
element necessary for the institution of political power, and that
is the consent of all the members. It is consent, and consent alone,
which can legitimize government (T2 §99).

Locke poses two objections to his consent theory. The first is
that there is no historical evidence of independent and equal
people convening to establish government in this way. He responds that this should not be surprising. Because of the primitive
conditions of early societies, written records are kept only after
government is formed. Nonetheless, it is evident that Rome and
Venice were formed by free and independent people. He cites
written testimony that in areas such as Peru, Brazil, and Florida
people on occasion chose their own leaders. Since reason proves
that people are naturally free and history gives examples of governments formed by consent, "there can be little room for doubt,
either where the Right is, or what has been the Opinion, or Practice
of Mankind, about the *first erecting of Governments*" (T2 §§101–104).
The second objection which Locke raises against his own consent
theory is that, since all humans are born into some kind of government, no one could have the liberty of uniting to form a new
and lawful one. The objection is refuted, he claims, by the plethora
of lawful governments that have existed since the beginning of
time and do exist at present. If the objection were valid, there must
be only one lawful government and then, adds Locke somewhat
sarcastically and not at all persuasively, all we would have to do
is identify it and give obedience to it. Moreover, "by the law of
Right Reason," children coming to maturity are free from parental
tutelage and can decide the political body to which they will give
allegiance (T2 §§113–18). As to the kind of consent necessary for
the establishment of government, Locke claims that there is general agreement about express consent. It is tacit consent that
causes difficulty. In practice, it is the owning and enjoyment of

possessions and land which are the main expressions of consent, both explicit and tacit. Moreover, express consent is perpetual, and the one making such a declaration cannot return to the state of nature unless the government is dissolved or the consenter is cut off from membership in the community. Those who give tacit consent may surrender their possessions, leave the common-wealth and enter into another, or begin a new one with others (T2 §§119–21).

Locke again appeals to natural law when he discusses legisla-tive power. Such power, as "the *first and fundamental positive Law* of all Commonwealths," is itself obliged by the fundamental natural law to preserve society and all its citizens. It is supreme, sacred, and unchangeable, and it cannot be usurped by any other person or power. At the same time, it cannot be absolutely arbi-trary but is limited, for it is derived from the consent of the people whose own power, also given by the natural law, is in turn limited. For example, they have no absolutely arbitrary control over their own lives or over the lives and properties of others. In short, the dictate of the law of nature continues when one enters into society; it equally binds individuals and legislators forever. Further, the law of nature is simply the expression of the will of God and is an unwritten law found in the human mind (T1 §§134–42).

One issue that was fiercely debated in Locke's time, and even much earlier, was the balance of prerogative and privilege. The Tory position was that legislative and executive power was in-vested by prerogative primarily in the crown, and the rights exercised by Parliament, for example, to levy taxes, were privi-leges granted gradually over several centuries. The Whig position was that the rights of Parliament, especially of the House of Commons, were constitutionally established centuries ago. This issue was another cause of contention, in addition to the religious conflicts, that led to the Civil War and the Glorious Revolution.

In dealing with prerogative in the *Second Treatise*, Locke does not involve himself explicitly in this dispute. Laslett maintains that the *Second Treatise* is unique among similar writings of his time, for it did not enter into the current debate about Whig liberalism or arguments from history for English liberty, Common Law, the House of Commons—all constitutional issues.[8] He was concerned more with general theory, and for this reason, claims

Laslett, his work has survived while those of some of his contemporaries have not. On the more general level Locke has in mind a government in which the legislative and executive branches are distinct, as in "all moderated Monarchies, and well-framed Governments" (T2 §159). Prerogative has to do with the discretionary power that a ruler possesses to make decisions not covered by existing laws and even contrary to them. He argues for the occasional use of executive prerogative based on the fundamental law of nature dictating that the good of society be preserved. At times this good can be hindered, for example, when situations arise that are harmful to the common good and when the legislature cannot be quickly convened. He is confident that the citizens do not object to this procedure when it is for their good and not detrimental to it. Locke conjectures that in an early stage of government laws were few and rulers more paternal, in which case the ruler had wide discretionary powers. But in time princes abused their prerogatives, and the people put metes and bounds upon them. In doing so, they cannot be considered to have encroached upon the ruler's prerogatives but only to have acted as rational creatures who are concerned with the common good (T2 §§159–64). Alluding to English history, Locke maintains that prerogative was most widely accorded to "our wisest and best Princes" who acted for the common good and received popular approval. Unfortunately, their successors, who were not so considerate, set a precedent by establishing a right to make use of prerogative even when it was harmful. The result was that the people were able to abrogate such prerogative only through conflict (T2 §§165–66). Locke takes up "the old question" as to who is the judge of the lawful use of prerogative. He seems to strike a pessimistic note by conceding that there is no remedy but "to appeal to heaven." But he adds that constant abuses can be so great that the people will find it necessary to remedy the situation (T2 §168). He will pursue this further when he states the conditions for the dissolution of government.

   Locke deals with two topics which indirectly affect the question of the legitimacy of a government, about which Hume will have a good deal to say. They are conquest and usurpation. He considers conquest because, during the frequent wars between European countries, many seemed to downgrade consent and to consider conquest an acceptable origin of government. Locke rejects the principle outright in the case of an unjust aggressor whom he likens to a robber entering a house by force and seizing another's possessions. The case is different regarding a conqueror in a just war. He has legitimate powers over certain people within the territory (T2 §§175–77).[9] Usurpation is the seizure of the power of government by certain persons within the commonwealth while the laws remain in place. It is unlawful because the right to name the persons who are to rule belongs to the people whose consent it was that brought the commonwealth into being. Therefore the right of the usurper to rule can be legitimized only by their consent.

The last two chapters lead up to the conditions under which government may be opposed and even overturned. These may occur in the case of tyranny, which is the exercise of power beyond what is right, that is, when the ruler acts for ambitious and selfish ends and when the abused have no recourse to law (T2 §§199, 207). But even here, Locke is careful to specify the conditions for opposing and dissolving an existing government. The unlawful acts should fall upon the majority of the citizens, or, if only upon a few, there should be good grounds for believing that they will eventually be applied to all; the people should be convinced in conscience that their laws, estates, liberties, lives, and religion are in danger (T2 §209). Locke gives a long list of instances in which legislative power, and executive power too, may be abused (T2 §§212–22). In sum, they consist in the endeavor "to *take away, and destroy the Property of the People*, or to reduce them to Slavery under Arbitrary Power." In effect, a state of war exists between government and the people, in which case all former agreements cease, the king is king no longer, and the people, whose right it was to establish the government in the first place, now have the right to establish a new government (T2 §§222, 235, 240, 243). Locke anticipates the objection that the people who are politically uninformed and prone to be contentious will continually attempt to overthrow the government. His answer is that in general people are slow to depart from established ways. England itself is witness to the fact that they have been long-suffering and that, in spite of revolutions, the realm has been maintained in its existing constitution with its kings, Lords, and Commons. Yet "a long train of

Abuses, Prevarications, and Artifices" will finally prompt the people to depose the government (T2 §§223, 225). Locke ends the *Second Treatise* with the "common question." Who is to judge when king or legislature has violated the trust committed to them? It is only reasonable to answer that the people themselves should judge, for it was they who entrusted them with the power to rule and so they should have the right to withdraw that trust when it has been betrayed (T2 §240).

Obviously much more could be said about Locke's views on the themes of the present chapter. The following will have to suffice by way of final comments. As already noted, the theory of natural law plays a central role in the *Second Treatise*. But in that work Locke seems to suppose that it has already been firmly established. I have argued that this was not done in the *Essay*. James Tyrrell, Locke's long-time friend, informed Locke in letters and personal conversation that the treatment of the law of nature in the *Essay* and *Two Treatises* was being criticized on the grounds that it was inadequate. Locke did not remedy the situation. Various reasons for this failure have been given by the commentators; either he felt that he had sufficiently justified it or he gradually became aware that natural law could not be demonstrated in terms of his own epistemology.[10]

I would like to suggest another reason. It seems to me that there was an ambivalence inherent in Locke's philosophical thinking. I would call him "an empiricist in transition," that is to say, he looked to past traditions and tried to incorporate some of their elements into his own intellectual framework. At the same time he was dissatisfied with some aspects of those traditions and sought to begin afresh. The ambivalence can be explained in large part by his intellectual background. As I indicated in Chapter 1, Locke studied Aristotle at Oxford, which would have given a rationalistic thrust to his philosophical viewpoint. At Oxford also he became a disciple of Robert Boyle, and this led him into chemistry and physics. Not long after, about 1666, he began to read Descartes. We know this from Lady Masham in whose household he lived during the last dozen years or so of his life. Lady Masham reported that, on Locke's own testimony, the first philosophy books that interested him were those of Descartes and that, though he had some differences of opinion with the French philosopher, he found his works highly intelligible.[11] Both rationalist and empiricist strains, then, influenced his early thinking.

This ambivalence is evident at the beginning of Book I of the *Essay*, which is an introduction to the whole work. He professes "to enquire into the Origin, Certainty, and Extent of humane Knowledge; together, with the Grounds and Degree of Belief, Opinion, and Assent." His will be "the historical, plain method" (EU 43–44). This means that he will reject any power of mind to form innate ideas, a task he undertook in Book I, and as he states at the end of that Book, he will ground his principles on an "*appeal* to Men's own unprejudiced *Experience*, and Observation" (EU 103). Yet in the preceding sentence, while warning the reader not to look for undeniable, cogent demonstration, he asks the liberty often assumed by others to take his principles for granted, but he confidently adds that he could demonstrate them, if need be. These texts reveal a tendency to both rationalism and a thoroughgoing empiricism and manifest a confidence that both strands can be reconciled. This may or may not be possible, but Locke himself failed to make the synthesis and this is no more evident than in his treatment of natural law. As a result, despite his frequent references to it in the *Second Treatise*, the principles and applications which he discusses are in fact based on "the historical, plain method"; that is, they are claims that he thinks reasonable people do make or should make about social and political arrangements. In other words, the positions he develops could have been adopted without reference to natural law.[12] I would suggest, then, that Locke's *Second Treatise* is an elaboration of civil law, which is the second of the three kinds of rules or laws listed in the *Essay*. It is the rule established by the Commonwealth to safeguard the lives, liberties, and possessions of those in political society. In the second *Essay*, he called it a division of the moral law. In the *Second Treatise*, he professes to establish civil law on the foundation of natural law, but he fails to substantiate his claim. Effectively, civil law is detached from morality in the strong sense in which he understands the latter term. His criteria for justifying his positions on political society are based, not on reason in the sense of natural law, but on criteria that a reasonable person would apply in making judgments. This does not mean that the latter kinds of judgments cannot be called moral, but they do not have natural law as their foundation, as Locke intended.

Let us now return to a problem that was initially raised in my review of the *Essay*. The point was made that his moral theory as seen in that work is open to the charge of individualism and self-interest. Is this true also of the *Second Treatise*? Surely rights of citizens and obligations of government are central to that work. As we know, human rights were the subject of philosophical and political writing and debate in England and France during the seventeenth and eighteenth centuries. There were increasing protests by the people against what they took to be the arbitrary use of power by rulers. These were issues common to Hobbes, Hume, and Rousseau, leading to the Civil War and Glorious Revolution in England and to revolutions in America and France, to mention some of the writers and political upheavals of that era. Locke was made aware of the political scene in England through his early acquaintance with Shaftesbury, so it is not surprising that he too was deeply concerned about rights and that it was a major theme of his political writing. In the light of the situation at the time, the *Second Treatise* can be read as a reasoned, one might even say reasonable, treatment of some potentially explosive issues.

But is this enough for an adequate social and political theory, if indeed, as Laslett suggests, Locke's position was not confined to specific historical events but had a more universal import? Was there sufficient attention given to the concerns of people not only as individuals protecting their own rights but as members of a community working together in mutual cooperation for common goals? Or was the emphasis on *my* rights in relation to yours and to the power of government? Indeed Locke often mentions the common good, and early in the *Second Treatise* he quotes a passage from "the judicious Hooker," whom he cites as stating that the equality of all people as human beings is the foundation of the obligation to mutual love among all and of the duties we owe to all others in justice and charity (T2 §5).[13] The quotation itself speaks of the love and affection all should have among themselves. But this high ideal, once enunciated, is not taken up in the rest of the treatise. The emphasis is on rights to be protected, means of accomplishing that end, conditions under which they may be violated by other members of society or by government, and action to be taken against the serious abuse of rights by rulers. It can be argued that Locke and other political writers of the time fulfilled a great service and no doubt they did. But Hume, while totally discarding natural law, gave greater scope to human relationships in his moral and political theory. Dewey had great respect for seventeenth- and eighteenth-century liberalism, but he argued that its failure to explore the social dimensions of the person, coupled with later social and economic conditions, led to the oppression of the individual which early liberalism had attempted to eliminate. But more about that in the following sections.

HUME

In the preceding section, I suggested that Locke could be called "an empiricist in transition." He still had an affinity with the past, and this was particularly evident in his retention of natural law. In Hume we have the complete empiricist, though the precise meaning of this term in relation to his moral and political theories must be clarified. Here natural law plays no part. I believe his break with religion had a good deal to do with this. Locke still referred to natural law as known through revelation or human reason. Hume, though raised as a strict Scottish Presbyterian, reacted against its strong Calvinism. Consequently in early life he gave up the practice of religion. It can be argued as to how much his later thought was influenced by his early religious experience.[14] But there is very little evidence of it in his moral theory. And so he works out a completely naturalistic ethics that does not depend either on the existence of God or on a belief in religion. Nor does it depend on reason either.[15] This follows, first of all, from the purpose which he proposes for moral theory. It is a practical, not speculative, discipline; it teaches us our duty by showing the beauty of virtue and the ugliness of vice and moves us to form habits by which we seek the one and avoid the other. Moral theory, then, aims at arousing the passions and affections, whereas reason discovers truth, satisfies understanding, and leaves the affections unmoved (T 457; EN2 172–73). He goes on to address more specifically the divisions of reason: Demonstrative reason has to do with the relation between ideas; moral reason,

with matters of fact. In this division, moral reason does not mean reason about virtue or vice but human judgments about factual matters (EN2 35, 164). Now, it seems at first as though Hume is developing an argument that is different from his position that moral judgments involve the passions while reason is detached and cannot move one to action. But actually, in order to appreciate Hume's rejection of both kinds of reason, it is important to realize that for him there is a quality distinctive of moral judgments about virtue and vice. It is the beauty and attractiveness of the one and the deformity and ugliness of the other. But that quality in turn is proper to sentiments and passions in the *mind* and not to *objects*. I shall develop this shortly. For the moment it is sufficient to keep this in mind in order to understand his rejection of reason. The following is an attempt to summarize the long and sometimes convoluted treatment that Hume gives to it.[16]

Demonstrative reason considers relations between ideas. These relations could be (*a*) between ideas in the mind, (*b*) between ideas of objects outside the mind, and (*c*) between an idea in the mind and an idea of an outside object. All of these fail to explain moral judgments. The first would not suffice, since then we could be guilty of vices within ourselves, whereas vice has reference to some situation in the outside world. Nor does the relation between ideas of outside objects meet the requirement, for if relations alone were considered, patricide would not differ from the case of a seed dropped from a mature tree that grows larger and destroys the parent tree; nor would incest differ in humans and animals. In the latter case, it is pointless to argue that an animal lacks reason and cannot appreciate the turpitude, for the supposition was that the morality consists in the relation itself. Third, a comparison between an idea in the mind and something outside could lead to a contradiction. Take the relation of contrariety; one could be harmed by another but return that action with kindness, and the action would be a virtue. On the other hand, the same person could be treated well by another but perform an unkind act in return and that would be a vice. In both instances, the relation was one of contrariety but with different results (EN2 288). Reason about a matter of fact does not help either, for Hume wants to know precisely what in the matter of fact yields beauty or ugliness upon which virtue or vice depend. Consider some vicious crime, such as murder. Examine the act as long as you wish, you will never discover vice. But look within yourself and you will find the sentiment of disapproval or blame in which alone vice consists (EN2 468–69).

There is one more possible way of explaining virtue or vice, namely, by showing that morality consists in the comparison of action with a rule of right. An action, then, would be considered virtuous or vicious to the extent that it is in conformity or discon- formity with the rule. But then how determine the rule of right? By reason? But that would be "fine reasoning," replies Hume a bit scornfully. For the rule to which actions are to be compared must itself be determined to be right by considering the moral relations of objects. But this would beg the question, since it would suppose the relations of objects to have moral import, something which reason cannot establish, as Hume claims to have shown (EN2 288–89). It follows from all this that Hume rejects both natural law and reason, the first by simply ignoring it, the second by detailed argument.

Hume is now free to develop his moral theory along empirical lines. In his view, moral distinctions are not discovered by original impressions or impressions of sensation but by impressions of reflection which for their formation still depend on outside obser- vation and experience. For example, one may perceive by an original impression a parent caring for a sick child. But one may go on to esteem and approve the act and designate it as virtuous. Why? Because the action arouses in the observer an impression of reflection, which is a pleasure or satisfaction of a particular kind. And the pleasure and the approval which it evokes constitute the moral judgment. In the beginning of the process, Hume remains within the framework of direct perception or impression of sen- sation, that is, one directly observes a particular event. But this gives rise to an impression of reflection, in this case a feeling of pleasure, admiration, or approval, which is itself the judgment regarding virtue. The judgment that a given act is virtuous is an immediate feeling of an internal sense akin to the appreciation of beauty (EN2 170). Or again, the judgment of virtue is a feeling of satisfaction in the contemplation of a person or act, and that feeling is our praise and admiration, indeed the moral judgment regarding virtue (T 471). In short, it is sentiment that determines morality (EN2 289).

Several points should be noted. First, there is a shift from original impressions or impressions of sensation to impressions of reflection or feeling or sentiments. These latter are given a central role in the judgment regarding virtue or vice. Yet the introduction of feeling in Hume's moral theory is not without precedent. We recall that for him belief is a *heightened idea*. In the *Treatise* he states that it is an idea with added force and vividness (T 96). In the first *Enquiry*, he expresses it more clearly. Belief is a forceful, lively perception of an object. It is not a different kind of idea, but it is the feeling accompanying it that differentiates it from other ideas (EN1 49). But in the end, belief is not the feeling itself but an idea enhanced by feeling. In Hume's moral theory, however, feeling or sentiment takes center stage and becomes the essential factor.

Hume's moral theory leads directly into his theory of the person, especially in its social or communal dimension. This will be explored further in his political theory. For the moment, several points may be noted. The first is that moral sentiment or feeling is rooted in human nature and is common to all human beings. It is like a universal principle, a common musical string striking a chord that produces the same harmony of praise or blame, approval or disapproval. It is not a question of how I respond to a given action in calling it virtue or vice; it is a question of how we react and agree in our reaction. Moral judgment is based on a consensus; we all agree in our moral judgment, at least generally and in the long run. And the reason for this consensus lies in the fact that we all share a common human nature and thus we react in the same way in being aroused to a feeling of pleasure or displeasure when confronted with a certain action and in giving our approval or disapproval. Another important aspect of sentiment is its social dimension. It is also called sympathy which includes a concern for others whereby I am delighted by their good fortune and saddened by their misfortune (EN2 219, 275). Hume states that this principle is at the heart of morality and is so obvious that there is no need to look for "abstract and remote systems." It is also fruitless to ask why we are concerned with others. In any science, we can go only so far in the search for causes, and we must finally settle on a general principle that is its own justification (EN2 219–20 and note 1).[17] Such is the case with sympathy for others.

Justice is an important virtue for Hume. This is so not only because it brings out some essential elements of his position on virtue but also because it serves as a bridge between his moral and political theories. For this reason it deserves extended treatment. But there are other reasons as well. Hume called justice an "artificial" virtue arising from particular circumstances without which it would not exist. This seems to make it different from other virtues. Also it is usually viewed as emphasizing self-interest. Hence I will try to show (1) that the term "artificial" does not differentiate or denigrate justice as a virtue, and (2) that justice is not confined to self-interest but ultimately is social and communal. In the process it will become clear how integral justice is to his political thought.

In connection with the origin of justice, Hume raises two questions, the first regarding the manner in which the rules of justice are established, and the second regarding the reason why we assign the idea of virtue to justice. Actually each of these questions has several important implications. Thus the first question is not dealing with the virtue of justice, but with the three *rules* of justice, that is, property or stability of possession, its transference by consent, and the performance of promises.[18] Also, the first question has to do with *natural obligation* which is not yet imbued with a moral quality. In my own interpretation, this really should be called *natural or physical necessity*, since human beings have no choice regarding the rules of justice if they wish to survive. The question here is how they begin to establish and conform to the rules of justice through physical necessity or need to survive. At this stage, self-interest has dominant though not exclusive influence. The second question concerns the observance of the rules of justice as a virtue and essentially as entailing *moral obligation*. The question here is how the observance of the rules of justice moves from natural necessity to moral necessity or obligation and how the observance of the rules also becomes a virtue called *natural justice*. At this stage, altruistic tendencies come forward.[19]

In order to answer the first question regarding the observance of the rules of justice, Hume describes the "savage and solitary condition" of primitive peoples before the emergence of society. Their wants and necessities are numerous and their resources are few. In this respect, humans are in a more disadvantageous position than animals, which are better equipped to survive on their own. The only remedy for these overwhelming obstacles is society, which enables human beings banded together to overcome them. And humans are aided in the formation of society by another "necessity," namely, the natural concern of parents for their children. Hume has already dealt with these tendencies in his treatment of passions (T 417, 439).

Human beings, then, are necessitated by their primitive condition to form a society, and this necessity is aided by the natural appetite between the sexes and the natural affection for their children. But there are two factors which militate against society. The one is our "natural temper" of selfishness, which tends to favor family, relatives, and close acquaintances and to ignore strangers (T 486–87). Hume points out that this temper is often exaggerated, and humans are sometimes made out to be monsters we read about in fiction. Common experience testifies that the selfless generosity existing between spouses and between parents and children can be found among people at large. Yet there are outward circumstances which accentuate human selfishness and limit generosity to those joined together by close ties. These circumstances are the instability and scarcity of possessions acquired through industry and good fortune. People are put into competition with one another for the goods of life, and this can lead to violence. It is natural, then, that they should favor their own, but this tendency poses a threat to society. Fortunately there is remedy, but it is derived not from nature, but from *artifice*. Through the experience of living in society, humans become aware of its advantages and are even pleased by human relationships. Moreover, they learn that peace and harmony are best achieved when individuals transcend their own interests and those of family and friends by entering into a convention whereby stability of possession is established and all are able to enjoy what they have obtained. All realize that this arrangement, rather than detracting from the interest of family and acquaintances, is actually the best means of protecting it. Thus arises the first rule of justice, which is property or stability of possession (T 487–89).

Hume, then, has answered his first question regarding the origin of justice, that is, the question concerning the manner in which rules of justice are established by the artifice of men. By way of summary: (1) Hume is speaking of the rules of justice, not the *virtue* of justice; (2) he has as yet explained only the natural or physical necessity of the rules of justice, or at least of the first rule; (3) the rules of justice come about by artifice or convention and do not arise directly from human nature.

Hume now addresses himself to his second question, which has to do with the reason why we annex the idea of virtue to justice and why we can speak about moral obligation. By necessity, individuals have moved from the family stage to the society stage. They have learned from experience that private interest and limited generosity, both of which include only family and close friends, are best served by observing the rules of justice and, in particular, property. This will do when society is small. But when it becomes a tribe or nation, our interest in others outside the circle of family and friends begins to fade. And yet, something curious happens. We find ourselves displeased when others violate the rules of justice and pleased when these rules are observed, even when we ourselves are not affected. We are concerned that our fellow human beings are harmed by the one course of action and benefited by the other. We call the former action vice and the latter virtue, and we apply these terms to our own acts as well as to the acts of other people. We are displeased when others are harmed and satisfied when they are benefited because of the sympathy we have for them, generating a sense of moral good and evil consequent upon justice or injustice, that is, upon the observance or violation of the *rules* of justice (T 498–99).

Hume concludes by stating that interest in ourselves, our families, and close acquaintances motivates us, even necessitates us, to establish the *rules* of justice. Once society is formed in accordance with these rules, we are motivated through sympathy with the plight of our fellow human beings to approve of actions that benefit them and disapprove of actions that harm them, that is, to approve of the observance of the rules of justice and to disapprove of their violation. Justice, or the observance of the rules, is then elevated to the status of a virtue and assumes a moral quality. Justice as a virtue is called "artificial" because it needs human convention or artifice to establish the rules of justice (T 499-500). It should be noted that what is at issue here is *natural* justice which is in operation before the establishment of government in a state or *civil* society, where civil justice then arises, as we shall see later.

At this point I would like to bring forward a statement made by Hume regarding the reason why we assign the idea of virtue to justice. The statement can be easily overlooked, but it should be emphasized because I believe it gives a different slant to the virtue of justice the one usually presented by the commentators. He maintains that the moral quality of justice, that is, the sentiment of right and wrong, can be better understood when it is examined in relation to the natural virtues. It can be seen that justice, which he has called artificial, differs not at all *as a virtue* from the natural virtues (T 498). The latter are called such because they do not depend on human artifice or contrivance. Examples of such virtue are generosity, charity, beneficence, friendship. But we note a surprising fact. In dealing with natural virtue, Hume spends as much time on justice, an artificial virtue in the sense described, and he uses justice as a primary example when explaining the origin of natural virtue. He stresses again the importance of sympathy or the feeling that all human beings possess. Justice, for example, is a moral virtue because it looks to the good of all. But the same may be said of the natural virtues. These are highly respected among the moral qualities and many are social virtues, since they contribute to the good of society. And again this extensive concern for society is due to sympathy (T 576–79).

In the course of the discussion, then, Hume has been showing more and more the similarity between the natural virtues and justice. It should be noted that here he is speaking not of the rules of justice but of justice as a virtue with a moral quality. The only difference between the natural virtues and justice is that the good resulting from the natural virtues comes to pass from a single act, while each act of justice has to be seen in a general context of action. For example, I may perform a particular act of kindness toward a particular person in need, such as giving alms. This would be the exercise of a natural virtue. But the observance of a rule of justice must be evaluated against a whole system of actions before it can be called a virtue or vice. An individual act taken by itself may seem to be wrong, when, for example, a judge takes money from a poor man and bestows it on a wealthy man, presumably because the former owes the latter a debt. Taken by itself, the action may seem harmful; but in the context of law and justice it is ultimately beneficial to society and is appreciated as such. Consequently our sympathy for others *naturally* gives the action a moral character (T 579–80). Justice, then, as a virtue is established in the same manner as the natural virtues.

Though Hume stresses the influence of sympathy, he anticipates a possible objection. The farther away people are from us, the less we sympathize with them and hence we can become unconcerned regarding their welfare. This seems like a formidable objection, and surely it is. As noted above, Hume recognized it already when he discussed the origin of the rules of justice in society. But he maintains that calm and reflective judgment can help to remind us that the qualities that we admire in persons closest to us are no different from those in persons more distant and remote. They are equally worthy of approval and approbation. In this sense reflection can overcome the partiality that we often extend to those nearest to us by recalling that the actions of all persons near or remote contribute to the good of society as a whole (T 582–84, 602–604).

Hume concludes Book III of the *Treatise* with a section that underscores important points made throughout his discussion of ethics. They have a particular bearing on our present subject. Sympathy is a powerful principle in human nature. It gives us the strongest sentiments of approbation; it is the chief source of moral distinctions; it operates in justice which is approved of only because it contributes to the public good. In brief, moral distinctions are derived from the affections, and the sense of morals can be attributed to an extensive sympathy and generosity inherent in our nature. This is true even of justice; though its origin is artificial, its moral quality is natural (T 619–20). Summing up what has been said about justice, the following points are clear: (1) Justice arises in society, first as rules or laws, then as *virtue*. (2) Justice and the natural virtues are the same as virtues, that is, as having a moral quality; they are also the same regarding the role that sympathy plays. (3) The artificial virtues differ from the natural in their *origin*, that is, in the former virtues artifice and convention give rise to agreements regarding ways of behaving. In the case of justice, this means an agreement to observe certain rules regarding property and promises. Insofar as these modes of behavior arouse sentiments of approbation or disapprobation, they are called virtues or vices. (4) The artificial and natural virtues differ also in the fact that the former operate in a system while the latter do not.

So far Hume has shown the origin only of natural justice, or the virtue of justice as it arises in society prior to the formation of government. The task at hand is to follow him in his explanation of how *civil* justice arises, or justice in a state. For the sake of clarity, it should be noted that natural justice, which includes the three rules of justice, exists in society before and after government is established. Civil justice consists in allegiance or obedience of the members to magistrates. And again Hume makes the distinction between natural necessity and moral obligation. He begins by recalling the previous difficulty regarding the limitation of generosity to family and close friends. He has already suggested how this difficulty can be overcome. Nonetheless as society grows larger and more complex, it is again subject to that tendency which is as inherent in human nature as sympathy, namely, a selfishness that is confined to nearest friends and present circumstances.[20] He calls selfishness an infirmity of human nature which is dangerous to society and seems beyond the possibility of being corrected. Steps can be taken to overcome one's natural infirmity by reflection, meditation, and continued resolve. But all this will be found to be ineffective. Since human nature cannot be changed, the circumstances must be altered by instituting government, the purpose of which is to guarantee the strict observance of the rules of justice (T 535–37). Government, then, arises by a natural necessity or artifice, just as the rules of justice did.

Hume now proceeds to explain how allegiance or obedience to government emerges as a moral virtue. As we have seen, human beings through self-interest and necessity enter into society and institute a convention or artifice to observe the rules of justice. Once society is formed, through sympathy they extend their concern to all members and approve of actions that promote public interest. Justice is then raised to the status of a virtue. A similar development takes place regarding allegiance. As society grows larger, the members are subject to the attraction of the immediate good over the mediate and greater good, and this threatens the very existence of society. Government is necessary in order to guarantee the observance of the rules of justice, among which is fidelity to promises. Allegiance, then, arises first from a natural or physical necessity. But once government is in place, the members approve of actions that further public interest, namely, obedience and loyalty to government, and disapprove of those that are prejudicial to it, such as disloyalty and sedition, inasmuch as all such actions affect the observance of the three rules of justice. In effect, then, natural justice and civil justice or allegiance have the same source, an artifice or convention arising from natural necessity. The origin of their moral quality is also similar in that the members of the community approve or disapprove of actions that further or hinder public interest (T 543–46).

A pressing difficulty, however, arises regarding Hume's treatment of the origin of government and the source of allegiance. Nothing is said about sympathy in these actions. They portray a view of human nature that seems far narrower, or at least less extended, than that presented in his treatment of justice and the natural virtues. But these sections do not negate everything else that he says about the outgoing tendencies in human nature. They, too, like the section on the origin of justice, must be read in the context of his earlier and later treatments of sympathy. His omission of an explicit reference to sympathy in his discussion of government can be due to the fact that he is supposing it and that he is now much more concerned with addressing himself to the political issues that were being debated between Whig and Tory and among philosophers regarding the state of nature, the origin of government, and the consent or contract theory. My thesis is strengthened by the fact that Hume's move from natural necessity to moral obligation in his discussion of government and allegiance in the state conforms perfectly to the move he makes in his treatment of justice in society. It is legitimate to suppose that everything said about the one, particularly about sympathy, pertains to the other.

When Hume's ideas are viewed according to the arrangement

that I am suggesting, his theory shows a remarkable order and consistency. He traces the development of man from a primitive stage, through "unpolished society," to a cultivated and complex state. And once the proper distinctions are made between artificial and natural virtue, and between natural and civil justice, his moral and political theories begin to emerge in sharper lines. We are also provided with tools in order to work through the charge that Hume's moral theory verges on the hedonistic, utilitarian, or whatever. Moreover it can be seen that Hume's theory of human nature is not atomistic, as it seems to be in his treatment of ideas and personal identity, but that it is open to interpersonal relationships leading to the formation of community and society. One may still feel inclined to question the validity of the arguments used by Hume to support his view of human nature and of the origins of society and justice, both natural and civil. But from my own reading of Hume, I do not think that he can be accused of developing an atomistic view of human nature. His final position is a balanced one. He can become almost ecstatic at times in his praise of sympathy and altruism, yet he is aware of the selfish tendencies in people. He sees in human nature a constant struggle between an interest in self and in those close to us and a concern for those more remote. In his view, we are powerless to overcome our selfishness except by contrivances, whether these be the laws of justice or the establishment of government. But once these are established, sympathy and moral sentiment, which are also parts of our nature, naturally come into play.

The discussion of civil justice brings us directly into Hume's political theory. My purpose is now twofold: the first is to pick up some issues raised by Locke and to note Hume's position on these issues; the second is to show how the notion of sympathy, which is central to Hume's moral theory, is continued in the judgments he makes on events in English history.

There are some striking similarities yet profound differences between Locke and Hume on the origin of society and government. Both begin with primitive societies which are formed out of the necessity to protect human rights, principally the right of property. Civil government is constituted to guarantee these rights. But there the similarity ends. Locke maintains that the initial rights of human beings are bestowed by the law of nature given by God, and it is the same law, under the impetus of necessity, convenience, and inclination, that drives people to form societies and then political communities. Government itself is constituted by the consent of the people. Hume opposes both these positions. The drive to society and civil government is founded in human nature but does not include natural law. Self-interest and sympathy, essential characteristics of human nature, are the originating and stabilizing influences of both society and government.

In rejecting the consent theory or original contract, Hume uses two arguments. He calls these by various names, but I will refer to the first as the "philosophical" argument, to the second as the "historical" argument. The philosophical argument is more theoretical and is based on an analysis of self-interest. The historical argument refers both in general and in particular to historical events. The philosophical argument depends heavily on Hume's analysis of the origin of justice, or more precisely the third rule of justice, namely, the obligation of keeping promises. As with all three rules of justice, the obligation to keep promises arises from self-interest. The generosity of individuals is limited to those close to them (T 519). However, from experience people learn that mutual assistance in time of need is obtained by promises to offer such help to each other. An important point is that the keeping of promises arises from self-interest and is needed for the survival of society. Equally important is his view that the rules of justice and their obligation precede government. It seems reasonable to conclude that government arises from the keeping of promises. Now, Hume is willing to concede that this may be the case in small and primitive societies. But it is false to conclude that all civil allegiance is reduced to the obligation of a promise and that consent alone binds citizens to their rulers (T 541–42). For in large civilized societies, the drive of self-interest makes it impossible for the members to observe the rules of justice without establishing government. Consequently both the necessity of keeping promises and that of establishing government derive from the same root, self-interest, but Hume insists on the difference and independence of each. Their ends and means are distinct; the adherence to promises is necessary for mutual trust and confidence among people in common life; obedience to magistrates is required to provide order and peace in the commonwealth. Hence the obligation of allegiance does not arise from promises (EN2 468).

Hume adds the "historical argument," though he calls it also an argument from "popular authority," which is different from "philosophical reasoning" (T 546). It is derived from history and experience.[21] Again he concedes an original contract *at first* in the most primitive of societies. The original records no longer exist. Even so, the consent was probably made during a war and continued as a matter of habit when hostilities ceased. Yet "philosophers who embraced a party," the Whigs, have gone on to assert that all governments owe their origin to such a contract and that the people are obligated by a promise. Moreover, the promise is conditional and lasts only as long as the ruler is just. To refute this claim, Hume bids his opponents to look at the course of history, and they will find no warrant for their position. Magistrates do not appeal to it but look to conquest or succession as a justification for demanding obedience. And by far the majority of the people of a nation would think it strange to be asked if they had promised to obey. They would reply that they were simply born to such obedience and have a moral obligation to submit to government because everyone thinks so. Both magistrates and people consider disobedience to be treason and rebellion and therefore subject to punishment. Moreover whether we look to Persia or China, France or Spain, Holland or England, even to the ancient Greeks who were the most democratic of societies, the result is the same. Hume adds that he does not exclude the consent of the people as one legitimate foundation of government. Where it has taken place, it is the best and most just. He only maintains that it has seldom occurred, and so we must look elsewhere for the foundation of government. Nor can the argument for tacit consent be sustained according to which some argue that, by remaining within the realm, one tacitly or implicitly approves the ruler. This has no weight, since peasants or artisans cannot make the choice to leave, being poor and knowing no foreign language. In some cases in history, princes have forbidden their subjects to leave (E 454–62; T 547).

Closely related to the question of the original contract is the problem regarding the right of citizens to overturn the government. In the *Treatise*, Hume first states the position of those who defend the contract theory. Since allegiance to government is founded on a promise, they argue, subjects are freed from allegiance to rulers who are guilty of flagrant violations of the rights of citizens. The latter freely submit to government in view of attaining peace and security, which the magistrate in turn pledges to guarantee. But if instead the union results in tyranny and oppression, the citizens are freed of their promise and may overturn the government. Hume maintains that "this conclusion is just, tho' the principles be erroneous" (T 550). He repeats his argument which shows that the obligations of promises and of allegiance to government, though originating from the same source, are independent. The first does not give rise to the second. Instead he proposes a principle "more immediately connected with government" which gave rise to government in the first place and which is the source of the obedience due to it. The principle is interest in the security and protection which political society provides and which sanction the authority of government over its citizens. If a ruler oppresses the people and destroys their security, he destroys also any bonds that existed between government and people. Some may counter that one is still bound in conscience to submit to a tyrannical government. Hume agrees that for the most part we should obey general rules even in exceptional cases. But if the exception itself is like a general rule and is grounded on very many common instances, the case is different. In the present situation, it is a common principle that human nature is open to unruly passions and is prone to prefer immediate interest over rules of society. This is true even of those selected for positions of power and authority. It is to be expected, then, that "excesses of cruelty and ambition" will occur. Hume concludes that our knowledge of human nature and our observations of history and experience allow exceptions and permit citizens to resist in good conscience the tyranny of rulers. Passive obedience, then, even under tyranny and oppression, is an "absurdity" and the contrary opinion "the most violent perversion of common sense" (T 549–52).

In the essay called "Of Passive Obedience," Hume defends the same position. Passive obedience in extraordinary cases is "a preposterous idea of the subordination of duties." But in this essay he nuances his position a bit and shows himself to be more cautious. In assessing the degree of necessity justifying rebellion, he confesses that he favors a tight bond between ruler and citizens which should be broken only in desperate cases. As reasons for his caution, he mentions the evils of civil war, the tendency of rulers to become even more tyrannical if they sense a spirit of rebellion among their subjects, and the advantage of inculcating obedience over that of studiously seeking out exceptions. For all that, he felt that passive obedience must be forthrightly challenged since there were those who propagated the opinion that there are no exceptions to obedience (E 474–75).

Having strongly affirmed the importance of rendering obedience to government, and having decisively rejected the original contract and the excesses of passive obedience, Hume states that "the next question is, to whom [obedience] is due, and whom we are to regard as our lawful magistrates" (T 554). In effect, he is proposing an alternative to the original contract. This question is treated at great length in the *Treatise*, III, II, xi. In sum, he gives five principles for answering this question: (1) long possession in one form of government, (2) present possession, (3) right of conquest, (4) right of succession, and (5) positive laws. A briefer statement of these principles appears at the end of the essay "Of the Original Contract." In both texts, the ultimate principle seems to be the peace and liberty, the interest and necessities of society (T 562; E 472). Hume makes some interesting and important points regarding the origin of all government. He regards it as certain that, with few exceptions, every government is founded, not on an original contract, but on conquest, usurpation, or rebellion, and that its title is "at first worse than doubtful and uncertain" (T 556; E 460). He adds that even in the case of a sovereign whose royal family can be traced back to the remotest ages, it is common for historians to find such origins (E 468).

But if sovereigns assume power under such violent conditions, what legitimates their rule? Why should they be regarded as lawful magistrates? Hume again has recourse to a principle that figured so prominently in his moral theory. It is sentiment, sympathy, or what he now calls the universal opinion of mankind. Though in the speculative sciences such as metaphysics, natural philosophy, or astronomy, an appeal to general opinion would be completely out of place, such is not the case in the present question. There is no other criterion. So strong is this criterion that the most decisive argument against the original contract is that it goes counter to the opinion, sentiments, and practice of people of every age (E 472–73).[22] In the attempt to defend his position, Hume makes an even stronger claim. Not only does popular opinion or sentiment have a high priority, but in cases such as this it is "in great measure" infallible, or, again, "perfectly infallible" (T 546, 552). It is rare that Hume can be caught making so strong a statement. It seems likely that, in his anxiety to refute what he took to be an erroneous and even harmful position, he overstates his case. He avoids this in his later treatments of this question.

Now that sentiment or popular opinion has been introduced into Hume's political theory, I shall follow him as he works it out, especially in his application of it to the events of English history. This can be clearly seen in the *Treatise*, Book III, and in the *Essays*. But the relevant passages focus mainly on the deposition of James II and the Hanoverian Succession of 1689. Further examples are given in *The History of England*. This is a massive work of six volumes covering the period from the invasion of Julius Caesar to the revolution of 1688 and the accession of William of Orange.[23] However my attention will be highly selective, focusing on those events about which Hume makes comments pertinent to the present topic. The historical period begins with the reign of Elizabeth (1558–1603) and ends with William. When this latter period is reached, the *Treatise* and the *Essays* will also be discussed.

In Hume's opinion, Elizabeth was the most popular sovereign in England's history (H IV:145). This was true in spite of the fact that hardly anyone before her and none after her stressed so strongly both in theory and in practice the authority of the crown (H IV:124). But Hume makes a significant statement when he gives as a reason for her popularity the fact that her policies, ideas, and actions conformed to the principles accepted at that time and to the general understanding of the constitution, so much so that no historian of that period even took notice of it (H IV:145). In Appendix III after his treatment of Elizabeth, Hume elaborates on these statements. He wanted to opposed those of his contemporaries who misread the actions of Elizabeth. Some praised her for granting liberties and privileges to the people. But in this they had no understanding of the decisions that she made. But there were others who went to the opposite extreme and criticized the queen for exercising authority contrary to the present ideas of a legal constitution.[24] In Hume's opinion, however, Elizabeth merely acted according to the prerogatives inherited from her predecessors. Moreover she was confident that her subjects approved the unlimited authority which she exercised.

Hume adds a further comment. When one considers exercise of power in particular instances, the primary question is: What is best? But when the question affects how power is distributed among bodies of a constitution, the question to be answered is: What is established? In other words, the latter question is asking what has been in effect over a long period of time, what has precedence, and, more important, what do the people of the time recognize as acceptable. This is in accord with Hume's principles concerning the obligation of allegiance to government. He emphasized universal or popular approval at a given time, and this took precedence over the manner in which the magistrate was able to assume power in the first place, even if the means was rebellion or violence. By this criterion, Elizabeth acted according to the course of administration acceptable at that time. Hume even suggests that her predecessors were more arbitrary than she was and that their subjects were more submissive than hers. At the same time Hume shows by his praise of Elizabeth that in his judgment her exercise of power was not only established but also best. The criterion of each is the same, namely, the acceptance by the people over a long period of time (H IV:354–55).

Hume takes a similar stance regarding Elizabeth's successor and the first of the Stuarts, James I (1603–1625). For example, in the matter of assessing duties for "tonnage and poundage" (for many years a nervous issue in English politics), Hume concedes that the power was originally subject to a vote of Parliament and was given for a limited period. In time, however, going back as far as Henry V (1413–1422), the authority was granted for life, and each prince gradually began to consider it as his inherited prerogative and the vote of Parliament as a formality expressing the will of the people (H V:41). As a result, when in 1610 James on his own authority changed the rates of customs, and even raised duties on some kinds of merchandise, it was a practice which, though looked upon as arbitrary and illegal in Hume's day, was quite acceptable in view of previous practice. Nonetheless Hume faults both James for not correctly assessing the growing spirit of liberty and also the Commons for being impatient and precipitous in making demands on the king when patience and gentleness could have achieved libertarian goals.

During the next decade the rift between king and Commons grew wider. In 1621, the Commons presented a list of grievances against the actions of the king, a bold step without precedent for many years and rare in times of peace (H V:90). James, of course, appealed to precedent and prerogative, and so the debate went on. In Note 1 of Volume V of the *History*, Hume again makes the point that, during the reign of the Tudors and especially of Elizabeth, the House of Commons had little influence. Hence James naturally followed Elizabeth's lead, which he considered to have popular approval (H V:558). Unfortunately he failed to realize his own limitations and the growing drive for civil liberty. Much of this is repeated in the appraisal of James's reign after his death in 1625. The House of Stuart inherited a monarchy invested with almost unlimited authority. But what was it that gave it credibility and compliance? Not money, for this was always in short supply. Not force, since the king had no standing army. Instead, the authority was founded on the approval of the people who in turn were following precedent and procedures of the past (H V:128). The people accepted it, and this enabled the government to hold their allegiance in spite of stress and strain during the course of history.

This theme of Hume's, by now becoming familiar, is repeated in his account of the reign of James I's son, Charles I (1625–1649). He sums up the situation as it had prevailed for almost three centuries. Frequently rebellious subjects had opposed the king's authority, though no one in peaceful times had challenged regal power on constitutional grounds (H V:179). But times were changing, and the rising spirit of liberty no longer tolerated the strong assertion of kingly prerogative. By 1640, discontent, which had been growing for some thirty years (roughly from the beginning of James I's reign) threatened the kingdom with some great upheaval. The boundaries between prerogative and privilege become more and more blurred, the king's arbitrary actions began to lose popular support, law and religion normally supported by judges and prelates had less influence on the people and even tended toward rebellion, the nobility became disenchanted, and the Commons was looked upon more favorably (H V:283). Added to this was the agitation of both English and Scottish Puritans who incited the nation with the drive for liberty and with their aversion for the Church of England.[25]

The subsequent history of Charles I's reign was a progressive series of attempts to appease the opposition by surrendering regal prerogatives. Hume has some interesting comments to make on these developments. For one thing, he mentions the decision to accede to the demand of Parliament to abolish many judicial courts, especially the Star Chamber which possessed many discretionary powers and had authority to punish violations of the king's edicts. On the one hand, he states that in making these demands Parliament was taking a risky, even rash, step, since history shows that in every government the magistrate needs some arbitrary power without which no government can survive (H V:329). In other words, *before* the event Parliament's decision could be judged as ill-advised. And yet, Hume admits, Parliament with some justification feared that the king would go to excess in the use of his authority. In the long run, however, *subsequent* events were to show that, though some inconveniences followed, the advantages overbalanced them, and so the English people should be grateful to their ancestors for taking the risk. In fact, with some exceptions, the actions of Parliament deserve now the praise of all lovers of liberty. Former abuses were remedied and steps were taken to prevent their future occurrence. It should be noted that Hume here makes explicit a principle latent in his account of Elizabeth's reign. It is the principle that public opinion, not only regarding circumstances *at the time* of public action but also regarding *later consequences*, determines judgments about the rightness or wrongness of a political act. This is so even if such action at the time was tainted with some inequity. The use of this principle will become clearer later. In any case, Hume sums up his personal assessment of Parliament's action with the following comment.

And if the means, by which they obtained such advantages, favor often of artifice, sometimes of violence; it is to be considered, that revolutions of government cannot be affected by the mere force of argument and reasoning: And that factions being once excited, men can neither so firmly regulate the tempers of others, nor their own, as to ensure themselves against all exorbitances [H V:330].

However, he maintains that the general question regarding the privileges of Parliament has been and still is "one of the greatest mysteries in the English constitution; and, in some respects, notwithstanding the accurate genius of that government, these privileges are at present as undetermined as were formerly the prerogatives of crown" (H V:358).

The story of the growing opposition to Charles I leading to civil war and the beheading of the king in 1649 is a familiar one. In his reflections on these events, Hume reviews the conditions for opposition to a monarch. He indicates that there should be a gradation of the severity of the abuses of power as one moves from resisting a king to dethroning him to executing him. He agrees that conditions could exist which justify the ultimate penalty—for example, in the case of the Roman Emperor Nero. But the great disparity between the characters of Nero and Charles I is obvious to all. Surely Charles went to excess in the use of his authority. Yet he was not entirely to blame for his own downfall. Hume claims that the madness and fanaticism of the people were also responsible (H V:545–46). It was statements such as this which drew upon Hume criticism from all sides because, as he notes in "My Own Life," he had "presumed to shed a generous tear for the fate of Charles I" (H I:xxx).

Hume's account of the Interregnum (1649–1660) contains little that is of interest for our present topic. Even in his account of the reigns of the restored Stuart line, Charles II (1660–1685) and James II (1685–1688), there is the repetition of the growing drive for liberty and the imprudent actions of the kings in meeting each emergency. If anything, these two monarchs were even more arbitrary and impolitic than the first two Stuarts. This is especially true of James II who was a Roman Catholic and took strong measures in support of his own religion. Finally opposition grew so powerful that James II could no longer maintain his authority and he was deposed. In 1689, after a long and bitter debate in both Houses, Parliament officially declared William and Mary as King and Queen of England.

Let us now review Hume's judgment on this momentous event, first as it is given in the *Treatise* and *Essays*. Regarding the deposition of James II, Hume in the *Treatise* first states a general principle that "in the case of enormous tyranny and oppression," it is lawful to oppose even supreme power with the force of arms. But in concrete instances, neither the laws nor philosophy can identify a particular rule for determining the rightness of resistance (T 563). Then how is the issue to be decided? His answer is that it was permissible for the Lords and Commons to depose a king, exclude his rightful successor, and choose another since the *judgment of the people* approved such actions. Regarding the accession of William of Orange, Hume states that at first it might have aroused some disputes and appeared to be challenged, but it now seems that his own claim and that of his three successors have "acquired a sufficient authority." A king may rightly be considered a usurper while he lives and be accepted as lawful ruler by posterity. Hume adds:

> Time and custom give authority to all forms of government, and all successions of princes; and that power, which at first was founded only on injustice and violence, becomes in time legal and obligatory. Nor does the mind rest there: but returning back upon its footsteps, transfers to their predecessors and ancestors that right, which it naturally accords to the posterity, as being related together, and limited in the imagination [T 566].

This discussion in the *Treatise* reveals an interesting aspect of Hume's use of common opinion to determine the rightness of political events. In his moral theory, sentiment or approval operates as moral judgment about a particular act at the moment when the act is performed, or shortly after that. But in his political theory, when he makes a judgment on the legitimacy of a government (in this instance, the Hanoverian Succession), Hume plays the role of a present observer making a judgment about a *past* event in the light of intervening historical developments. Thus he can say that, though William could be considered an unjust and violent usurper when he ascended the throne in 1689, he with his ancestors and successors could now, a half-century later, be accepted by the people as being in the lawful line. The mind retraces its footsteps, and the imagination unites all members of the line so that all are judged lawful. Hume notes that "time and custom give authority to all forms of government, and all succession of princes." In this section, he does not indicate any actions on the part of the Hanoverian rulers which would please the people and render them benevolent to their new rulers. There is the merest hint of this when he refers in very general terms to the fortunate results that the revolution had for the Constitution (T 563). But he does not develop this.

In his essay "Of the Protestant Succession," Hume again takes up the accession of William of Orange and his successors. At first it seems as though he will modify his former perspective and make a judgment about the matter based on the evidence available *at that time*. He puts himself in the place of a member of Parliament at the beginning of the reign of William and Mary, and he weighs the pros and cons. Should the king and queen be declared legal, or should the House of Stuart be reinstated? He summarizes arguments for each position. On behalf of the Stuarts, one could argue that the people in general (consensus again) are more ready to accept the direct successor to James II, and this gives peace and stability to the nation. On the other hand, the Stuarts enlarged their prerogatives and exceeded the limits placed on rulers. In addition, the Stuarts were partial to Roman Catholicism, and this fact is fraught with dire consequences. This religion is intolerant; it separates the sacerdotal and regal offices and bestows the former on the pope. Besides, the whole temper of the people is aligned against the Popish Church (E 496–97).

For the Hanoverian line, it could be argued that the Prince of Orange stood ready to accept limitations on his prerogatives. His selection would extinguish the hopes of other pretenders waiting in the wings for the opportunity to gain the throne and to disrupt the peace of the nation. On the debit side, the Prince has ties with foreign nations that are hostile to England, and this could involve her in many disputes. After recounting the advantages and disadvantages of each claimant, Hume favors the Hanoverians.

> The princes of that family, without intrigue, without cabal, without solicitation on their part, have been called to mount our throne, by the united voice of the whole legislative body. They had, since their accession, displayed, in all their actions, the utmost mildness, equity, and regard to the laws and constitution. Our own ministers,

our own parliament, ourselves, have governed us; and if ought ill has befallen us, we can only blame ourselves [E 498].

Now, there is something curious about Hume's line of argument here. His initial standpoint was to have been that of a member of Parliament wrestling with the question at the time of decision. One, of course, could question whether William engaged in no intrigue, cabal, or solicitation to gain the throne, and it is certainly an exaggeration to say that his selection was approved by a "united voice" of Parliament. But this aside, the crucial aspects of his argument, that is, William's track record and that of his successors, report not a struggle of conscience in 1689 but the considerations that one would make in the eighteenth century, some fifty years *after* the fact. Again, as in the *Treatise*, Hume is using hindsight in judging the rightness of a past act in the light of subsequent events.

Hume follows a similar line of argument in the *History*. He points out that James II committed a fatal error in failing to realize that the approval of lawyers and past theorists was not sufficient to sustain a prerogative. If the general opinion of the people condemned it, the use of prerogative would be looked upon as blatant injustice and usurpation (H VI:482). Again it is the general opinion of the people that constitutes the most important criterion for judgments on public policy. Regarding the Hanoverian Succession he states that, though normally such changes are accompanied by great violence and disorder, such was not the case. Everything proceeded with great tranquillity, and the people universally accepted, that is, approved, the change of regime (H VI:528–29). As an aside, one could ask if a revolution and invasion could be called a process of "great tranquility." But in any case, Hume's *History* too cites the favorable events that followed the revolution and the new monarchy. In a ringing paragraph, he states:

The revolution forms a new epoch in the constitution; and was probably attended with consequences more advantageous to the people, than barely freeing them from an exceptional administration. By deciding many important questions in favor of liberty, and still more, by that great precedent of deposing one king and establishing a new family, it gave such an ascendant to popular principles, as has put the nature of the English constitution beyond all controversy. And it may justly be affirmed, without any danger of exaggeration, that we, in this island, have ever since enjoyed, if not the best system of government, at least the most entire system of liberty, that ever was known amongst mankind [H VI:531].

At this point, some concluding remarks may be in order, if not overdue. One aim in the discussion of Hume's moral and political theories was to show the central role of sentiment or sympathy in these theories and also his social or communal view of human nature. It was seen that the judgment regarding virtue is not an act of direct perception or of reason but of feeling, sentiment, approval. By the time Hume reaches his political theory, sentiment, now regarded as universal opinion, becomes the criterion for judging whether a general principle or a particular action is justifiable or not.

Finally, in the discussion of Locke, I suggested that his political theory, despite its frequent references to natural law, is actually based on criteria that reasonable people would use in making political judgments. This is even more true of Hume. In addition, Hume's criteria have close links with his empirical epistemology, whereas the empirical foundations of Locke's political theory are quite nebulous.

And yet there are problems that can be raised regarding Hume's criteria for moral judgments. I have already indicated my discomfort with his position that *subsequent* events can determine the correctness of a political action that *at the time* was judged wrong or at best highly suspect. This would mean that the bloody and unprovoked invasion of a country by a usurper could be justified if eventually the situation of the conquered was considered to be improved. Or a vicious act of murder could be judged morally acceptable if subsequently the spouse of the deceased received a large inheritance. At the very least, Hume's moral theory does not exclude these possibilities. His criterion for virtue is approval of actions which in the long run benefit society; therefore on his terms the kinds of acts just mentioned as well as his judgments regarding events in English history can be morally justified. Even if Hume held that the end justifies the means, as his position seems to suggest, he gives no clear guidelines by which one would evaluate the end that could justify such acts.

NOTES

1. *Essay*, Book II, Chapter XXI. Locke's notion of active and passive powers has already been examined in Chapter 2 above on cause and effect.

2. This thesis is developed by John W. Yolton, *John Locke and the Way of Ideas* (London: Oxford University Press, 1956).

3. The edition used is John Locke, *Two Treatises of Government*, ed. Peter Laslett (London: Cambridge University Press, 1988). All references are taken from the *Second Treatise* and are included in the text as T2 with paragraph number.

4. Laslett describes this influence. See ibid., Introduction. pp. 25–37.

5. See Paul Langford, "The Eighteenth Century (1688–1789)" in *The Oxford History of Britain*, ed. Kenneth O. Morgan (New York: Oxford University Press, 1988), pp. 393, 403.

6. This theme has been admirably developed by Kenneth L. Grasso in "The Emergence of the Liberal Doctrine of Toleration in the Thought of John Locke" (Ph.D. diss., Fordham University, 1988).

7. James Collins, *A History of Modern European Philosophy* (Milwaukee: Bruce, 1954), pp. 360–61.

8. Laslett, *Two Treatises of Government*, Introduction, pp. 75–79.

9. I shall not follow Locke in his complex and sometimes ambiguous distinctions regarding the kinds of power the conqueror has over the various classes of people within the realm. See T2 §177ff.

10. For differing views on this point, see Laslett, *Two Treatises of Government*, Introduction, pp. 79–82; Grasso, "Emergence of the Liberal Doctrine of Toleration," pp. 413–22; John Dunn, *The Political Thought of John Locke* (Cambridge: Cambridge University Press, 1969), p. 187. It should be noted that during the 1660s Locke wrote a series of papers on the law of nature which were never published during his lifetime. They were finally published by W. von Leyden as *John Locke: Essays on the Law of Nature* (Oxford: Clarendon Press, 1954). These essays were Locke's most extended attempt to give rational justification for the law of nature, but they were not consistent with his later empiricist epistemology and metaphysics.

11. See Aaron, *John Locke*, p. 99; Cranston, *John Locke*, p. 100.

12. There is a difference of opinion regarding the relation between Locke's *Essay* and his political works. On the one end of the spectrum, Grasso argues that the *Essay* was written for the express purpose of giving a philosophical basis for the political writings; see "Emergence of the Liberal Doctrine of Toleration," esp. pp. 378ff. Laslett, on the other hand, claims that the *Two Treatises of Government* is not at all an extension

of the philosophy of the *Essay* into the political arena; see *Two Treatises of Government*, Introduction, pp. 82–83. Though each argues his point well, I do not think that either one has settled the question.

13. Richard Hooker (1554?–1600) was an Anglican divine who "taught theology to the majority of English Churchmen." Cranston, *John Locke*, p. 125. Laslett discusses "Locke's Use of Hooker" in the Introduction to the *Two Treatises of Government*, pp. 56–57. In a footnote to §5 of the *Second Treatise*, Laslett further indicates Hooker's influence and adds that Locke's frequent references to him in the *Second Treatise* were intended "to lend respectability to his position and to turn back the flank of his opponents, especially the good churchmen amongst them."

14. Norman Kemp Smith discusses this point. See David Hume, *Dialogues Concerning Natural Religion*, ed. Norman Kemp Smith (New York: Bobbs-Merrill, 1947), Introduction, pp. 1–24.

15. See *Treatise*, III, I, i and ii; *Enquiry 2*, Section I and Appendix I.

16. Hume's discussion is not clear, and I have given my own interpretation of his meaning.

17. See also *Enquiry 2*, p. 293, and *Treatise*, p. 471.

18. Though Hume lists three rules of justice, only the first and third will be considered in this context.

19. There are two terms which Hume frequently uses in the *Treatise* and about which there is a good deal of ambiguity. The first is "natural" and the second is "moral obligation." To understand what Hume means by natural, one has to understand the meaning of that to which he opposes it in any given context. Thus he opposes natural to artificial, moral, and civil. These oppositions are discussed in relation to justice. Hume has very little to say about moral obligation in the *Treatise*. He does not explain precisely what it means. In discussing justice, I shall occasionally use the term moral obligation where Hume does, though at other times I will substitute terms like virtue or moral quality. In Chapter 6, I shall return to moral obligation.

20. Throughout Hume's discussion, one notes a constant tension between self-interest and sympathy for others.

21. David Hume, *Essays Moral, Political and Literary*, p. 461. References to the *Essays* are included in the text as E with page number.

22. A careful distinction must be made between the original contract or consent and general opinion or sentiment. The former is a consent, explicit or tacit, given by the people to the ruler at the beginning of the formation of government or early on. Hume holds that there is no such consent, except perhaps in primitive societies. The right of the magistrate to rule is established for the most part by conquest or usurpation or both. General opinion is the acceptance by the people at large regarding the decisions and actions of the magistrate. As history develops—and this

would apply especially to England—there is a kind of dynamic relationship, sometimes even conflict, between king and people. In his *Essays Moral, Political and Literary*, Hume examines many aspects of government, but two ingredients relevant to the present discussion can be identified. The one (treated at length in this chapter) is the opinion or consensus of the people. The other is the need of moderation in disputes arising between king and people and between the two parties, Whigs and Tories. The ruler must have the ability to maintain a proper balance between the prerogatives of the crown and the privileges of the people, while at the same time he must elicit the people's consensus and support. In Hume's opinion, Elizabeth had this ability while the Stuarts did not.

23. Hume published the *History* between 1754 and 1762. He began with the Stuart reigns, then went back to the Tudors, and finally to the Roman occupation. The splendid Liberty Classics edition, published in six volumes in chronological order, is based on the posthumous edition of 1778, the last to contain corrections by Hume. It provides a long-needed edition of the *History*. All references to the *History* are taken from this edition and are included in the text as H with volume and page number.

24. This, of course, involves the constitutional issues regarding the antiquity and status of both the prerogatives of the crown and the privileges of the House of Commons. My interest centers on the criteria which Hume proposes to settle debates on these issues.

25. In Hume's view, the Puritan movement and its conflicts with the crown had a considerable influence on political events as early as the reign of Elizabeth. I described these conflicts, as related by Hume, from James I to the Civil War and the beheading of Charles I in 1649. See my article "David Hume on Religion in England" in *Thought*, 66 (1991), 51–64.

5

MORAL, SOCIAL, AND POLITICAL THEORIES: THE PRAGMATISTS

IN THE PREVIOUS CHAPTER, the philosophy of the empiricists fit neatly into the areas designated by the title of the chapter. The case is a bit different with the pragmatists. Peirce did not develop an ethics in the usual meaning of that term. His approach to the self has only recently been examined carefully, and he has little to say regarding political philosophy. James gave no extended treatment of ethics, though a moral theory can be constructed from this writings. He is often criticized for an excessive individualism, but I shall fulfill the promise made in Chapter 3 and try to show that he did have something to say regarding the social dimension of the self. A political theory is hardly mentioned in his philosophy. Dewey, however, is a notable exception among the three pragmatists, since he fully developed a moral theory, the social dimension of person, and a political philosophy. Not only that, all three areas are closely integrated. The purpose of this chapter, then, is to take the pragmatists in turn and to examine what they had to say in their own areas.

PEIRCE

To say that Peirce had no moral theory in the usual sense of the term may meet with the objection that there is no "usual" sense and that ethicians have developed a moral theory in various ways.

Yet there are some family resemblances that characterize moral theory. It is a practical discipline having to do with conduct that is judged to be right or wrong in accordance with some norms. The norms either are derived from God or are grounded in what is considered proper for a human being to do. The conformity or disconformity with the norms is called virtue or vice. Finally, some kind of sanction, reward or punishment, is judged proper in the case of those who conform to or violate the norms. These approaches to ethics, then, include a theoretical component, that is, general norms, and a practical component, that is, the application of the norms to concrete situations, the designation of virtue or vice given to various acts, and the imputation of moral sanction.

Peirce's theory of ethics departs from these characteristics in a number of ways, so much so that it is scarcely recognizable as a moral theory in any usual sense of the term. For all that, it will be helpful to examine it because it not only brings out the unique character of his approach but also enables us to see it in relation to that of the other philosophers whom we are examining. Actually it would take a whole chapter and then some to elaborate fully Peirce's approach to ethics, but it will have to be stated as briefly as space permits.[1]

The unique character of Peirce's ethics can be more easily appreciated if one understands the meaning he gave to philosophy and to the overall purpose of his philosophic enterprise. Familiar is his description of philosophy as "the attempt of a physicist to make such conjecture as to the constitution of the universe as the methods of science may permit, with the aid of all that has been done by previous philosophers" (CP 1.7). He includes philosophy under the heading of theoretical science, along with mathematics and the physical sciences. The whole temper of his philosophy is indicated when he calls it a "serious research" grounded in logic. He maintains that his philosophy cannot be understood by those unable to reason exactly, "'which alone is reasoning.'"[2] His own background consisted in being steeped in the physical sciences, while his intellectual framework was fashioned through long hours in the laboratory (CP 1.3–4). He judges that "the present infantile condition of philosophy" stems from the fact that it has not been pursued by people so trained. Peirce has high standards for the philosopher, and he classes as a mere beginner "in the case of an educated man, one who has not been seriously, earnestly, and single-mindedly devoted to the study of it for more than six or eight years" (CP 1.134). But in calling philosophy a science, he does not mean that it conforms to the laboratory conditions of the natural sciences. Instead it utilizes "those universal experiences which confront every man in every waking hour of his life" (CP 1.246). But that which should characterize the scientist, and hence the philosopher, is "a passion to learn," a single-mindedness, a desire to find out, a love of truth (CP 1.11, 43, 149). Philosophy ought to be studied in the same spirit as every science ought to be pursued, namely, "the spirit of joy in learning ourselves and in making others acquainted with the glories of God" (CP 1.127). So strongly did Peirce stress the theoretical aspect of science and philosophy that he excluded direct utility as its main purpose. Truth should not be sought in order to make money, to amend one's ways, or to help other people. He concedes that those who follow these goals may be better human beings, but they are not truly scientific (CP 1.45). In this he aligns himself with Aristotle, "a thorough-paced scientific man" (CP 1.618).

Why was Peirce so demanding in this view of the purpose of philosophy? One answer surely is that he himself had a passion to learn, to find out. And that by itself is enough to engage one's energies for a lifetime. But there are other reasons as well. He was afraid that, if the sciences are directly applied to concrete problems, then pure science will be diluted. He claims that the "infantile condition of philosophy" during the preceding century is due to the fact that it was not pursued by those trained in the scientific laboratory but by those in "theological seminaries" who were distracted from theoretical questions and were more concerned with practical applications to religion and ethics. The implication seems to be that their lack of scientific training led them to make serious mistakes in these areas. He does not deny that philosophy may be applied in this way but "only with secular slowness and the most conservative caution." He adds that he may be mistaken in his view, but he feels obliged to be perfectly honest in stating that his philosophy is not directly aimed at producing better or more successful people (CP 1.620–21). Another reason for his opposition to direct applications to practical matters is that science in America was being reduced to "pot-boiling arts" (CP 1.670). One can fault Peirce for exaggerating the situation and for minimizing the great advances made and to be made in technology. Yet he could also be called prophetic since he was able to foresee the preoccupation of technology with conveniences and utilities, while America lacked great creative minds who could make major breakthroughs in the solution of theoretical problems upon which technology depends. In any case, whether one agrees with him or not, Peirce fiercely maintained that interest in practical problems and in developing technological utilities was prejudicial to science. Science is a study of "useless things," and to set great minds to work on practical affairs "is like running a steam engine by burning diamonds" (CP 1.76).

This description of Peirce's vision of philosophy leads into his conception of ethics. In his early years, he took it to be a practical science involving rights and duties. As we have seen, philosophy for him uses ordinary experiences of everyday life. If this is the case, then it is natural to think that ethics should attend to rights and duties and therefore requires deep reflection on one's total experience over the whole of life. It also requires a knowledge of the society in which one lives. After further consideration, he began to realize that ethics should not be concerned merely with the conditions for achieving a definite purpose or with the question as to whether this or that action is right or wrong, good or bad. There is a prior question: What is the good? What is the ultimate reason beyond all reasons for calling this or that action right or wrong, good or bad? What is the reason "back of every reason" (CP 1.577)? Or to put it another way: "the fundamental problem of ethics is not, therefore, What is right, but What am I prepared deliberately to accept as the statement of what I want to do, what am I to aim at, what am I after? To what is the force of my will to be directed" (CP 2.198)? As I understand him, Peirce is pushing back to the ultimate question beyond all questions, the answer to which is to give meaning and guidance to all other questions.

Peirce makes the same point from another direction when he discusses "Ideals of Conduct" (CP 1.591–615). Everyone has ideals of how one ought to act in a manner befitting a rational human being in accord with particular conditions. These for the most part have been learned in childhood and they affect conduct in three ways. First, one performs a certain act because it is esthetically pleasing. It satisfies the agent at a given time. Second, consistency of ideals may influence conduct since inconsistency tends to repel the intelligent agent. Last, one projects the consequences of carrying out ideals and asks questions about the esthetic quality of the consequences. Through further reflection on these ideals, one sets up, even if vaguely, some rules of conduct and as a result one becomes disposed to act according to them. In the light of further experience, a person will subject accepted ideals to a re-evaluation so that there is a growth of illumination amid a variety of experiences. But as a reasoning being, the human individual engages in a theoretical inquiry, and begins to ask "what the *fitness* of an ideal of conduct consists in, and to deduce from such a definition of fitness what conduct ought to be" (CP 1.600). Again, as before, Peirce is looking for the reason or ideal beyond all others which indicates what ought to be done. In other words, he is asking about the "admirable without any reason for being admirable beyond its inherent character." This is not a practical question but a question about the "aim of all endeavor. The object admirable that is admirable *per se* . . ." (CP 1.612–13).

The crucial problem now is to identify what Peirce takes to be the ultimately admirable, the highest goal. In one place he calls it "the development of concrete reasonableness" (CP 5.3). By this he means that the *summum bonum* does not consist in action (and here he has in mind people like James and Dewey) but "in that process of evolution whereby the existent [Secondness] comes more and more to embody those generals [Thirdness] which were just now said to be *destined*, which is what we strive to express in calling them *reasonable*" (CP 5.433). This brief sentence expresses Peirce's evolutionary ontology and cosmology which view the universe as advancing from pure chance to pure law, though, of course, his fallibilism envisions this final stage as being approached asymptotically over infinite time. This is a large topic which cannot be fully treated here. Something has already been said about this in Chapter 2 on necessary connection where it was seen that Peirce's universe was an ordered one with powers in objects to operate in regular and predictable ways. The highest good beyond all others is the gradual working out of the evolutionary dynamism of the world toward more ordered activity. The role of human beings is to use their intelligence in seeing the universe to its completion. Hence he closes the section on "Ideals of Conduct" with the following statement: "Under this conception, the ideal of conduct will be to execute our little function in the operation of creation by giving a hand toward rendering the world more reasonable whenever, as the slang is, it is 'up to us' to do so" (CP 1.615).

This vision of the universe, its destiny, and that of human beings is an esthetic one. Peirce felt that such a vision was the only one that made sense out of the process of science, evolutionary theory, and human aspirations. As with so many other terms, the word esthetic took on a meaning peculiar to himself. At the same time, it has some analogies with other uses made of it. One speaks about esthetic appreciation which is often claimed to need no further justification. One appreciates, admires, approves, enjoys, feels pleasure in certain situations. As we have seen, this was central to Hume's moral and political theory. From that point of view, Peirce's use of esthetics has some resonances with these descriptions. Yet there the similarities cease. He admits that for a long time he had neglected esthetics, or, perhaps better, he had limited his understanding of it to the usual manner of considering it as having to do with beauty and ugliness (CP 2.199). If this were the case, he maintained, there could be no science of esthetics, for it had to do, with taste which is purely subjective (CP 2.156) and about which there could be no dispute (CP 5.111). This tendency to conceive the beautiful in relation to taste is a subtle and ineradicable narrowness characteristic of most of modern philosophy (CP 5.128). Though he considered himself still to be "a perfect ignoramus in esthetics," he claimed to have some capacity for esthetic appreciation. But he now became convinced that particular enjoyments must likewise answer the question regarding their ultimate validity. Esthetic enjoyment becomes for him the appreciation of that which is the justification of all feeling, "a sort of intellectual sympathy, a sense that here is a Feeling that one can comprehend, a reasonable Feeling" (CP 5.113). In fact, he concluded that esthetics had to do not only with questions of feeling, but with questions regarding the ultimate meaning, the highest good, the *summum bonum* beyond all reality.

It is now possible to return to the original question regarding the nature of Peirce's ethics. On the negative side, it is not a practical science; it does not have to do directly with action or with right or wrong, pleasure or beauty in the usual sense of these terms. On the positive side, ethics supposes esthetics, whose province is "to determine by analysis what it is that one ought deliberately to admire per se in itself regardless of what it may lead to and regardless of its bearings upon human conduct" (CP 5.36). Then ethics has to do with "right action which is conformity to ends which we are prepared deliberately to adopt," in conformity, that is, with the admirable in itself as discovered by esthetics (CP 5.130). It also attempts to free ethics from its excessive dependence on or its reduction to pleasure and feeling. His intention is not to eliminate all feeling, even pleasure, but to place them under the direction of the ultimate goals, which esthetics in his sense points out (CP 1.615).

For all that, it is not easy to immerse oneself in his ethical theory, resting as it does on his meaning of esthetics. Ethics, like philosophy itself, is for Peirce a theoretical discipline, and one inevitably gets the feeling that it has been over-intellectualized. In his esthetics, he has taken a stance directly opposed to science and evolution as it emerged in the America of his day and of the following century. He attacked exaggerated necessitarianism in science, the elimination of final cause, and the stress on efficient cause. For him, evolution has a purpose though it does not proceed according to unchanging laws. He opposed a chance universe and argued that it is a cosmos, operating in predictable ways. Law, then, was an objective factor in the behavior of things. His redefinition of esthetics too has a stuffy air about it and seems to reveal him as one who is unaffected by the beauty so abundantly evident in the universe. However, his stage of "musement" in his "Neglected Argument for the Reality of God" shows that he is a keen observer of nature and open to its wonders.[3]

His restriction of ethics to a theoretical science too can alienate many contemporary ethicians. Ethics has long been considered to be a practical subject, concerned with virtue and vice, right and wrong. The most important ethical problems are debated in the arena of particular conduct, under the influence, to be sure, of general principles. Peirce makes ethics so theoretical as to be seemingly useless for real-life situations that agonize for an answer. Peirce, I feel, would never deny that ethics can or even should be applied to practical problems. Therefore they are immediately applicable. What he opposed was the tendency to address such problems without sufficient thought being given to the rational principles that should guide action. This tendency would leave ethics open to taking its norms from subjective feelings of pleasure and pain, satisfaction and dissatisfaction, or from the ways of acting that are accepted in society at any given time. Nonetheless, he did have some wise things to say about how humans ought to act, and this leads us into his social theory and into the little that he has to say about political theory.

In Chapters 1 and 2 of this volume on experience and necessary connection, Peirce's notion of synechism was discussed. He applies it also to his position on the self in a section entitled "Synechism and Immortality" dated 1892. He begins by saying that the Greek meaning of the word is "continuous." He states that he had been developing the idea over many years, and he intends it to apply to all areas of experience (CP 7.566). Synechism rejects dualisms of every kind, which means not that individual things cannot exist but that they are not isolated, discrete "chunks of being" (CP 7.590). This applies also to the self whose completeness in some measure includes one's neighbors. I take him to mean that the ongoing interchange of ideas, interests, and activities with other people is an important element in constituting the self. Likewise, all human beings, since they share the same human condition and similar circumstances, make up "in a measure" each individual self, though neighbors do so more intimately than those more remote (CP 7.571). Peirce speaks of a "social consciousness, by which a man's spirit is embodied in others, and which continues to live and breathe and have its being very much longer than superficial observers think" (CP 7.575). He extends consciousness to the "spiritual" level in which the self becomes one of the "eternal verities" embodied in the universe as a whole. In the next world it will be fulfilled in "a spiritual embodiment" which in a way has already begun in this life (CP 7.575–77). This is heady stuff indeed. One need not follow him all the way in his attempt to extend his idea of connections beyond individual human consciousness to someone or something beyond this life. But he is surely on the right track when he states that synechism forbids us to affirm that the self is completely isolated or that it has no connections as a self with others (CP 7.571).

Peirce opens up a more definite and clearer avenue of approach to self in his discussion of language and communication. In the chapter on personal identity, I criticized Vincent Colapietro for his attempt to defend a substance theory in Peirce. At this point, however, I shall draw on some informative insights of Colapietro's, in his book on Peirce and the self. Colapietro follows Peirce's account of how humans develop language.[4] A child is first attentive to external objects—a bell that rings or an object that can be moved. The child then becomes conscious of his or her own body, which now becomes important, makes connections between certain spoken sounds and certain bodies, and learns a language. Peirce claims that the youngster's efforts to understand language are instinctive, and so the child learns to carry on a conversation. But the child learns more than the connection of words and objects; the testimony of others also teaches the hard lesson of error and ignorance when, for example, a hot stove is touched contrary to the warning of another. Self-awareness has begun to dawn. Colapietro states that the important point in this example is that the child becomes not only self-conscious but also community conscious and sees the self as "distinguishable but not separable from others; indeed, the identity of the self is constituted by its relations to others."[5] This is so because the child has learned a language, has entered into dialogue with others, and is put into contact with the world.

Peirce developed the social self more fully in his discussion of science when he indicated the manner in which it should be conducted (CP 7.5–54). Science has been successful because scientists put aside their own selfish aims, engage in cooperative discussions and efforts with others, inform one another about their progress, learn from one another's failures, and together reach solutions to new problems. Through it all, the researchers engage in the enterprise less for themselves than for future generations, whether it be in the use their successors can make of their discoveries to uncover new truths, or in enabling future scientists to reach solutions which they themselves sought but had not achieved. It is striking how one's view of Peirce can change after reading this account of how scientists should operate. His description of science and philosophy could lead one to suspect that he viewed the person as isolated and detached not only from practical affairs but from other human beings. But the Peirce we see now is one who, while maintaining the theoretical character of science, envisions it in terms of a spirit of cooperation among scientists, all of whom submerge their own particular interest in a concern for future generations.

Peirce did not confine the social dimension of the person to the highly theoretical enterprise of research. He meant to apply it more widely when he said that "man's highest developments are social" (CP 6.422). This statement, though brief, indicates Peirce's conviction that the self can be fulfilled only in association with other human beings, resulting in their mutual growth as persons. This point is brought out even more clearly in a footnote to his statement of the pragmatic maxim as formulated in his article "How to Make Our Ideas Clear" (CP 5.402n2). He does not want the maxim to be reduced to "a sceptical and materialistic principle," applied in too individualistic a sense. It has a relational quality as well. It may indeed be the case that many people cannot do anything more than to provide the bare necessities of life for themselves and their families. But it would be cruel to condemn them for, in spite of their "miserable littlenesses," they contribute to the collective endeavor of enabling civilization to reach its final outcome. This, he claims, is but another application of his "great principle of continuity" which sees all things as fluid and intimately connected. Applied to the human level, it means that persons are potential members of society and will not be whole if they remain isolated. "We are all putting our shoulders to the wheel for an end that none of us can catch more than a glimpse at—that which the generations are working out."

Peirce reserves his most eloquent passages on the social nature of the self for sections of a long piece called "Evolutionary Love." Personal growth comes only from love, which consists in striving to fulfill the highest aspirations of the beloved. It means that one sacrifices one's own perfection for that of another. He claims that the love so described is the ultimate expression of his synechism (CP 6.287–90). In another place, he states that love alone can be the motive of those who practice heroic deeds, for example, by dedicating themselves to the care of lepers. He further suggests that in turn the final explanation of such love can be found only in a belief in God (CP 6.502).

In "Evolutionary Love," Peirce comes the closest to giving expression to a political philosophy, as slight as his remarks may be. As the nineteenth century gradually closed (1892), he called it "the Economical Century." With biting sarcasm, he states that intelligence has been put to the service of greed to guarantee "the justest prices, the fairest contracts, the most enlightened conduct of all the dealings between men, and leads to the *summum bonum*, food in plenty and perfect comfort." But for whom? "The greedy master of intelligence." Greed has become "the great agent in the elevation of the human race and in the evolution of the universe" (CP 6.290). Such strong language is rare in Peirce and is reminiscent of Thoreau. One wonders what kind of moral, social, and political theories he would have developed had he thought of them in their usual meanings.

JAMES

Discussions of James's moral theory usually begin by noting that he never fully developed such a theory and explicitly discussed ethics in only one place, his 1891 address to the Yale Philosophical Club, "The Moral Philosopher and the Moral Life." But as a matter of fact large portions of his philosophy were devoted to showing that a human being is a moral person and that the world itself is a moral universe. But before considering his ethics, it would be helpful to examine further his notion of person. The chapter on personal identity dealt with James's critique of Hume. We shall now look at Peirce's criticism of James regarding the broader meaning of person.[6] Since James is perennially accused of subjectivism in his epistemology and theory of God, it is not surprising that such a charge should be brought against his view of person.

A text of James from the *Principles* is quoted by Peirce (CP 8.81–82). The full text is as follows:

No thought even comes into direct *sight* of a thought in another personal consciousness than its own. Absolute insulation, irreducible pluralism, is the law. It seems as if the elementary psychic fact were not *thought* or *this thought* or *that thought*, but *my thought*, every thought being owned. Neither contemporaneity, nor proximity in space, nor similarity of quality and content are able to fuse thoughts together which are sundered by this barrier of belonging to different personal minds. The breaches between such thoughts are the most absolute breaches in nature [PP 220–21].

In opposition to this, Peirce claims that observed facts reveal the contrary and hence James's view is "metaphysical speculation." He asserts that James goes beyond observation and espouses isolation due to a confusion of thoughts with feeling qualities. Of course, concedes Peirce, some small particulars can be isolated, but James exaggerates them and sadly misconstrues personality. The implication seems to be that for James the self is basically an isolated, private individual.

Now, several things may be said regarding this reading of James. First, it is necessary to place the text quoted from the *Principles* in the proper context. In previous chapters, James had discussed various theories of mind: the "automaton" theory, which viewed states of consciousness as epiphenomena running alongside brain events mirroring them exactly; the "mind-stuff" theory, which reduced consciousness to atoms associated together in various combinations to form distinctly sensible feeling; the "material-monad" theory, which attributed to each brain cell its own individual isolated consciousness, while the various conscious states are combined in an "arch cell" or external medium. In addition, as I have shown previously, James directly confronted the atomism of Hume. In view of all this, it is understandable that James's reactions against these mechanistic and atomistic models led him to stress the deeply personal character of one's own consciousness, hence not just *thought*, or *this* or *that* thought, mechanically and impersonally combined with others, but *my* thought or thoughts, conscious states that are personal in a living awareness of the self. In this regard, James as a psychologist was facing a specific set of problems which required a decisive answer.

Moreover, to call James's self an isolated individual is to neglect Chapter X of the *Principles* where James considered the self "in its widest acceptation." James enumerates various "selves": the "material self," which includes our own body and physical surroundings, such as clothes, immediate family, home, property; the "social self," or our relations with other people such as parents, friends, teachers, associates in professional life, and especially persons we love; the "spiritual self," or some central principle of thought, activity, spontaneity; the "potential social self" extending not only to potential others but even to God (PP 280–86, 300–301, 315–16). These considerations show clearly that James's person is not isolated within a private sphere but extends outward in manifold relations which in a real sense constitute and define the person. Of course, this is substantiated also on epistemological grounds for, as we have already seen, experience, inquiry, knowledge are essentially interactions between self and some aspect of the environment. In the following sections on his moral theory, other dimensions of the person will become evident. The above was meant to respond to specific criticisms voiced by Peirce.

The focus of attention in this section on ethics will be on the 1891 essay "The Moral Philosopher and the Moral Life" and the last lecture of *Pragmatism* (1907). Despite all that has been written about these selections, there are still some valuable nuggets to be mined from these two passages, not the least of which is the relation between James's moral and religious philosophy. There are several Jamesian notions that will be presupposed though not developed since they are well known. The first is human freedom, which James defended against determinism in his 1884 essay "The Dilemma of Determinism." Furthermore, in places too numerous to cite, he held that the universe is ongoing, unfinished, malleable and that intelligent inquiry and scientific methodology can alter and direct the future course of experience and events. This means that humans can assume responsibility for the future. In effect, this ability can be considered to be the most important characteristic of the Jamesian person.

As singular and isolated as "The Moral Philosopher and the Moral Life" seems to be, it deserves careful examination.[7] It was composed a year after *The Principles of Psychology* (1890) and before *The Varieties of Religious Experience* (1902) and *Pragmatism* (1907) and bears traces of these works, especially the latter two. In the first sentence James states that "the main purpose of this paper is to show that there is no such thing possible as an ethical philosophy dogmatically made up in advance" (WB 141). This sounds simple enough, but as a matter of fact he is doing much more than that. Surely the statement taken by itself is simply the application of his general epistemological position that there are no unchanging absolute principles, truths, ideals imposed upon concrete facts and experiences to which the latter must conform. This is consistent with his rejection of idealism and espousal of empiricism. Significant, however, and even outrageous for his times, is his assertion that ethics should be subjected to the same experimental, scientific methodology as any truth-claim. In this he anticipated Dewey's position, likewise looked upon as outrageous, that the scientific method should be applied to morals. As we shall see, however, James is much more restrictive than Dewey in equating moral theory with scientific method. In any case, a few sentences later James proposes what I take to be an even more important aim of his paper, namely, "to find an account of the moral relations that obtain among things, which will weave them into the unity of a stable system, and make of the world what one may call a genuine universe from the ethical point of view" (WB 141).

James states that in ethics there are three separate questions that must be asked. The first and for many the only one is the *psychological* question, which inquires about the origins of moral ideas and judgments (WB 142–45). Theologians answer it by postulating a "conscience," which is an intuitive faculty informing us about right and wrong. In opposition to this, there is the "popular-science enthusiast" who derides such "apriorism" and claims that moral judgments are derived from bodily pleasures and pains. James pays tribute to philosophers like Bentham, Mill, and Bain for making a contribution to moral discourse by relating moral theory to pleasures and pains, but he adds that something more must be considered to account for the "directly felt fitnesses between things." Such are "the feeling of the inward dignity of certain spiritual attitudes, as peace, serenity, simplicity, veracity; and the essential vulgarity of others, as querulousness, anxiety, egoistic, fussiness, etc." The appreciation of the nobler sentiments is a matter of taste and is due to "an innate preference of the more ideal attitude for its own sake" (WB 143).[8] Not even so-called good consequences can change one's conviction that some actions are mean and vulgar. For example, one would feel horror if an innocent person were to be tortured permanently so that millions could be happy. Such moral sensibility cannot be explained by any "laws of association" or corporeal pleasures or pains.

The second or metaphysical question has to do with good, ill, and obligation (WB 142, 145–50). Suppose the case of several individuals living in proximity. "Antique sceptics" have held that there is no objective criterion for moral judgment but only a wide variety of individual subjective opinions. A thinker who has any hope for a moral philosophy will not accept this supposition. He would hold that there must be some truth or authority to which all are obligated "so that system and subordination may reign." To find that ideal, the philosopher must trace the "ought" to some existing consciousness beyond which the philosopher cannot go (WB 147). And what would that consciousness be which can oblige others to conformity to a rule that it establishes? The answer is clear if there be a divine thinker. The deity is the model and source of obligation. But James presses the matter further and in doing so he remains faithful to the opening statement of his paper. Even if a divine consciousness exists, one need not, indeed should not, have recourse to some "abstract moral order in which the objective truth resides." The reason James gives is that obligation requires a claim made by some existing person. He holds that it is a superstition to suppose an "overarching system of moral relations, true in themselves" (WB 148). James acknowledges that this position may be difficult to accept since we are accustomed to suppose something called "validity," "moral law," or "metaphysical Being" existing above and beyond the concrete facts. If a divine consciousness exists, there is no need to refer to some *a priori* ideal in order to back up the claims made upon us by a deity. James's position here is a bit puzzling. There seems to be a conflict between his proposal of a deity and his rejection of an absolute ideal. A plausible explanation is that he wants to keep the door open for a belief in God which he will try to justify more fully at the end of the essay; at the same time he is faithful to his position that there are no absolutes. These two positions are not inconsistent since he holds for a finite God.

The third, or *casuistic*, question concerns the degrees of goods and ills so that the philosopher may put obligations in some hierarchical order (WB 142, 151–59). For the moment James sets aside a belief in a divine thinker and notes that there is much disagreement about what truly constitutes goods and obligations. But he again refuses to take the skeptical attitude and to hold that all claims are of equal worth. In one sense, the ambiguity and conflict about goods and ideals are muted, since we are born into a society that already accepts a hierarchy. "In other words, our environment encourages us not to be philosophers but partisans" (WB 154). Still, the philosopher who claims to be objective wants to avoid two extremes: the one would be to suppose some moral "schoolmaster" or "pontiff" telling us what are goods and which ones should be preferred in case of a conflict of goods; the other extreme would be to fall back on skepticism and to consider all claims to be of equal worth. James then proposes that the guiding principle for the moral philosopher is "to satisfy at all times *as many demands as we can*" (WB 155). This seems to be a utilitarian principle based purely on quantitative considerations. But his examples show that his goods and ills are chosen on qualitative grounds. In responding to the psychological question, he had listed goods and ills based on some internal sentiment, for example, peace, serenity, and veracity, or anxiety and egoism. Here he lists polyandry, polygamy, slavery, and license to kill as actions to be avoided. James maintains that moral theory resembles physical science in that both take certain hypotheses as normative which further the progress of the discipline and eliminate those which are detrimental. Ethics resembles physical science in another way as well. Its conclusions are never absolute, final, or detached from concrete facts. But there the comparison ends. For the ethical philosopher seeks something more, namely, the "most organizable" good that can enter into a more complex combination and become integrated into a "richer universe," a more inclusive whole. Yet it is not possible beforehand to know with certainty what kind of universe would fulfill these conditions, and in this regard James is faithful to the aim proposed at the beginning of his essay, which was to reject an ethical theory dogmatically made up in advance (WB 157–59).

Let me summarize James's position as developed so far. In accord with his epistemology, he holds that no ethical ideal is absolute or unchanging. There is room for new ideals in the light of further experience. The moral philosopher, then, should be open to this possibility. But while he refuses to close off the avenue to new ideals, he does not mean that all proposed ideals should have equal status. He first refers to a person's innate feeling that some actions attract and others repel. Though he dismisses the intuitions of the "divines," he claims that bodily pleasures and pains alone cannot explain our innate responses. Pursuing the problem of finding some norms that would mediate between absolutism and skepticism, he asserts that the existence of a God provides the model and source of good, ill, and moral obligation. But again there is no overriding absolute ideal acting as the needle of a compass pointing in the right direction. The fact that James's God is finite prevents his position from being inconsistent. Lastly, in addressing the problem of a hierarchy of goods, James proposes one way out, that of accepting the standards of the society into which we are born unless and until there is reason to alter or reject them. He compares this to the practice of physical science to this extent at least, that it admits no absolutes, accepts the hypotheses that have been tested, and remains open to new possibilities.

In "The Moral Philosopher and the Moral Life," the possibility of a deity enters the discussion early but only to show how ethics would be affected *if* there was a God. But toward the end of the essay, James brings forward his religious philosophy as the crowning point of his ethical theory (WB 159–62). Here we should remind ourselves of positions he has already developed and will develop more fully in subsequent works: human freedom, the universe as unfinished and malleable, and the possibility of humans taking responsibility for the future. But now he effectively introduces another question which asks what is required to inspire people to strive for the "most organizable good" and the "richer universe." It is "the strenuous mood" which motivates them to try to ensure that higher ideals will prevail, such as truth, freedom, and justice, and thus contribute to a more fulfilling life. James states unequivocally that this requires "metaphysical and theological beliefs," more pointedly a belief in God. A world without God, a "religion of humanity" (WB 150, 160), would not be sufficient motivation to further the ongoing progress of the universe and humanity since several questions would go unanswered. Why *should* we strive for the improvement of the lot of future generations? We do not love those who are remote from us in time, whose situation will most likely be much more felicitous than our own, whose health and material condition will be improved considerably. "No need of agonizing ourselves or making others agonize for these good creatures just at present." But a belief in God opens up entirely new perspectives. Sympathy for others is extended; the more imperative ideals assume new meaning and objectivity and sound "the penetrating, shattering, tragically challenging note of appeal" (WB 160). Religious faith inspires us with the courage to undergo misfortunes and tragedies. It also meets the demand of the philosopher for a stable and systematic moral universe that is in accord with freedom, a changing world, and the innate drive of the person for an answer to the ultimate question of the meaning of life. We may not fully know where God is leading us but that in itself is the stimulus to continue the quest.

It is easy to dismiss the final pages of James's essay as mere rhetoric, and undoubtedly some of it is. But the whole essay must be seen in the context of his constant preoccupation with religion and his serious attempt to justify a belief in God. It is interesting to note that the present essay preceded by five years his more famous "Will to Believe" published in 1896. This interest in religion continued throughout his major works to the end of his life. It would take too long to repeat a detailed examination of James's argument for God.[9] At the heart of it is his conviction that belief in God gives meaning to one's life while a rejection of a deity leads to pessimism and despair. This theme is evident in "The Moral Philosopher and the Moral Life," especially in the last few pages. It is James's answer to the question: Why should a person, even with a belief in God, strive for the good of human kind and of the universe now and for the future? One would like to say that love of and sympathy for human beings were his leading inspirations. Certainly in his personal life he was most considerate of others. To cite only a few instances: he made several unsuccessful attempts to obtain a permanent teaching position for his friend Peirce. He also tried to mediate disagreements and hostilities between some of his colleagues.[10] In *Pragmatism*, he derides Leibniz for arguing that ours is the best possible world, even to the point of asserting that souls damned for all eternity count for almost nothing compared with all the goods of the universe. James asks how this can be reconciled with a story in the newspaper about a poor laborer who cannot work because of illness and commits suicide rather than see his wife and six children without home and food (P 20–21). In "The Moral Philosopher and the Moral Life," there is one mention of sympathy for others, but it does not figure prominently in the present context (WB 160). The more direct link is between obligation as discussed in the "metaphysical" question and the claim put upon us by God. He speaks about "imperative ideals," about facing tragedy "for an infinite demander's sake," and about "a divine thinker with all-enveloping demands" (WB 161–62). It is possible to interpret these phrases to mean that one adopts the moral life under an imperative imposed by God since he already stated that obligation requires a concrete person making a claim on humans (WB 148). If this interpretation is correct, James is saying that one has the obligation to be moral, or in effect to be morally responsible for the universe, because God orders it. But I am not persuaded that he means it in this way. He does not mention an order, a command coming from God. Rather, God is the objective model of how one ought to guide one's life if it is to be worthwhile, the inspirer for persons to assume the strenuous life. In a sense this can be called a claim, a demand to which one is obliged. But it is such only to the extent that it is an invitation to abide by the demand and to live a life that is inherently rewarding or to reject the demand and to become disappointed and disillusioned. In true pragmatic fashion, one refuses to accept a moral life and a moral universe at one's own risk.

A similar line of thought is developed in the final lecture of *Pragmatism* called "Pragmatism and Religion." This lecture attempts to show that pragmatism is the "happy harmonizer" between the tough-minded empirical temperament and the tender-minded religious one. At this point in *Pragmatism*, James feels that he has justified belief in God as a philosophically respectable option. But it is not the God of monism, for he has already rejected such a deity on philosophic grounds, that is, an unchanging God as author of a preordained universe with absolute ideals. He proposes a pluralism, by which he means a finite God who produces a universe that is in the process of developing. The Jamesian problem is to inspire others to accept the strenuous life and to take responsibility for the betterment of the human condition and the improvement of the universe at large. In what again seems to be a rhetorical flourish, he poses a hypothetical case. Suppose God were to put the challenge to us: the world that I have created is not certain of being saved, but it can be if all cooperate to the best of their ability. There is real risk and real danger; success is not certain. James then speculates regarding the response that would be made to this challenge. He would have us believe that most people are "normally constituted" and have "a healthy-minded buoyancy," prompting them to accept the challenge. There are "superhuman forces also, such as religious men of the pluralistic type," and here he seems to mean people around us who are already believers and who are making heroic efforts on behalf of others. God too is our helper who, though finite, is superior to humans and is *primus inter pares* (P 143). Of course, some perhaps would not heed the call, for in any group of people there are "morbid minds" who are not inspired by such an invitation. They prefer to rest back on a religious and moralistic monism which gives assurances and comfort in the thought of a universe that cannot but be saved (P 140).

In this final lecture of *Pragmatism,* James seems to want the response of individuals to an uncertain outcome to depend on the strenuous, buoyant mood that thrives on risk and uncertainty, somewhat like the attitude of the mountain climber or space explorer. To a certain extent, this may be so. In James's own life, as we know, on two occasions he seems to have overcome depression, discouragement, and despair by making up his mind to reject such moods and by adopting a hopeful attitude. It is as though he decided that one either goes insane or elects to make something of one's life, even though the outcome is not certain. But I believe that these periods were also incentives for him philosophically to examine the world in which he lived. On philosophic grounds he rejected monism and chose pluralism. It is ultimately the reason why he thinks a positive answer to God's challenge is the only reasonable one. For the world of uncertainty as proposed by the deity is precisely the world we actually inhabit and the one that makes sense in our lived experience (P 141). He is already convinced that a belief in God and in a life of dedication to the salvation of the universe is the only one that satisfies the human drive for fulfillment. But again, the completion of our hopes and endeavors is not assured. That is the heart of his pragmatism, or as he variously calls it, his pluralism, his religious pluralism, his moral pluralism.

By way of a postscript, two final observations may be made. At the risk of stretching a point, I would suggest that there are some similarities between the moral theories of Peirce and James. First, neither developed an ethics in the "usual" sense of the term. They made few judgments on the rightness or wrongness of concrete human actions. Instead they developed the larger picture as a guide for responsible decisions. Peirce called it "concrete reasonableness," while James referred to the "most organizable good" that would fit into a "richer universe" or a systematic inclusive whole. And both opted for a belief in God. Furthermore I have protested against the attempt to reduce James's person to an isolated individual, and I have argued that it is essentially relational, extending in various ways to the universe and to other human beings. And yet I would admit that James does not develop a philosophy of community to meet the challenge of saving the world. His "metaphysical and theological beliefs" for the most part provide the motivation for that task. As we shall see, it will be left to Dewey to go beyond both Peirce and James in developing a social philosophy and in working out an ethics or religion of humanity. Dewey's political philosophy explores in detail an area that Peirce and James left practically untouched.

DEWEY

Perhaps the best way to begin a discussion of Dewey's moral theory is to quote two definitions given in the Introduction to the 1932 revised edition of *Ethics* by Dewey and Tufts. Ethics is defined as "the science that deals with conduct, in so far as this is considered as right or wrong, good or bad." Again, it is stated that "ethics aims to give systematic account of our judgments about conduct, in so far as these estimate it from the standpoint of right or wrong, good or bad" (LW 7:9). Attention will be given first to his meaning of morality, value, and the good. Dewey makes a distinction between customary and reflective morality (LW 7:171). The former is an accommodation to social usage whereby one conforms without question to the standards and rules of conduct that are generally accepted in a given society. Reflective morality arises when there is a conflict of goods and one needs to search for a reasonable principle to decide which course of action should be followed. This situation has roots in the general pragmatic position that inquiry begins in doubt. As long as nothing occurs to disrupt our beliefs, we remain content. But when doubt arises, we must initiate a method of inquiry to remove the doubt or to modify or change our beliefs in the face of new facts.

For Dewey, reflective morality is intimately related to goods, ends, purposes (LW 7:284–85). All of us are subject to the desire for certain objects and to the impulsion of immediate needs. Many different kinds of objects appeal to us on various levels without any reflection on our part. They attract us, they please us. In a sense, they can be called goods and values because we prize them. They can also be called ends, to which we tend. About these it can be said simply that values are values and nothing more need be added. There can be no doubt that such things are valued and desired. But the question is: Are they valu*able*, desir*able*? Are they truly worthy of being valued and desired? *Ought* one to value and desire them? As indicated above, these questions arise only when there is cause to doubt an affirmative answer to these questions or when one has to choose among several values not all of which can be chosen at the same time. It is at this point that reflective morality arises and that one enters into the process of criticism.

This brings us to the question as to how one distinguishes between the valued and the valuable. Dewey maintains that one cannot answer the question merely by examining what people do in fact desire. One must test the reasonableness of the object desired. He directs attention to acts that involve *relations* or *connections*, whether these be immediate or remote, and not to acts that are considered in isolation (LW 7:168–69). The point made here is that value, the end, the good, is relational, consisting of connections. Thus Dewey's value theory must be seen against the background of his assertion that all objects in reality are intrinsically connected, and in this view he took issue with empiricism regarding a description of facts or the given. He accuses the empirical tradition of particularism in that it dismisses connections and continuities as having any bearing on reality. On the contrary, relations are not purely subjective in the sense that only ideas are related, as Hume claimed. Knowledge has to do with related objects, and it is only in relation that the qualities of existing things are known. According to this view, an element such as hydrogen can be described not only in terms of its ability to combine with another element to form water but also in terms of consequences following upon other modes of conjoint activity. On the widest level, description and understanding of reality are commensurate with the entire range of such activity. Moreover, since "dynamic connections are qualitatively diverse," so-called degrees or levels of reality are understood and explained according to the range and complexity of interactions between things. In fact, knowledge of objects is possible only in terms of the connections between things and between things and the knowing subject. In short, then, Dewey claimed that the "predilection for ultimate and unattached simples" on the part of the empirical tradition left us with isolated, detached, self-sufficient data or essences. But he was equally critical of idealism and rationalism which, he claimed, accepted the basic atomism of reality and saw the need of some outside source to bind things together. Dewey maintained that intrinsic relationships did away with trans-empirical connectives. Hence he rejected both empiricism with its "stubborn particularism" and the opposed rationalism with its attempt to save continuities by "hyper-empirical Reason."[11]

Though Dewey's position included all levels of reality from humans down to inorganic matter, he frequently drew upon biological data and used the living organism to explain various aspects of his philosophy. The biological model is found in his major works on art and esthetic experience and especially in his theory of inquiry where this model introduces the entire discussion of these topics. The living being depends for its very existence and development upon its interchanges with the environment, and these interchanges are not external but internal and intimate. For example, breathing, drinking, the ingestion of food can exist only through relationships between organism and environment, and they can be explained by a description, not of the organism alone or of air, water, or food alone, but only of their natural interactions. In fact, the meaning of such things as organism, air, and food requires both poles and their interactions.[12]

But, as Dewey notes, all this is merely a starting point for discussing the value of the "social," which denotes specifically human forms of grouping and which is "philosophically the inclusive category." By inclusive he means that in general humans share the same condition as all other objects, that is, they exist and grow as humans only in relation with other objects in the environment—minerals, plants, animals, humans. But more than that, it is a distinctive mode of association and "the richest, fullest and most delicately subtle of any mode actually experienced." This means that humans are not merely added to physical and organic phenomena. These latter are actually modified in the relationship, and things themselves are qualitatively transformed. Examples would be land, natural resources, and forms of energy. On a higher level, physiological factors such as sex, procreation, immaturity, and need of care take on quite different characteristics when they involve humans, while at the same time relationships within the human family are different from those of animals.[13]

The most distinctive relationships are those existing between and among human beings. Persons grow and develop as humans; in other words, they achieve their true end, value, good, to the extent that they cooperate in shared activities for the welfare of all. To be human is precisely to contribute to the building of a community. In *The Public and Its Problems*, Dewey defines this as "conjoint activity whose consequences are appreciated as good by all singular persons who take part in it, and where the realization of the good is such as to effect an energetic desire and effort to sustain it in being just because it is a good shared by all" (LW 2:328). We have, then, Dewey's criterion for the true or reasonable good. Does the object or action contribute to the welfare of others? If it does, it is not only valued but valuable, not only prized but appraised, not only an object of desire but a true or reasonable good. For Dewey, then, the good is that which contributes in some way to the welfare of others. There are, of course, ever wider and more inclusive modes of association. Hence the more that individuals commit themselves to the welfare of others and the wider the range of activities which are engaged in in this enterprise, the more good do they achieve and the higher will be the moral quality of their actions and of their whole character. They will then attain happiness, which is a stable condition of peace and inner contentment through interest in others and in whatever contributes to their development. Or, as Dewey expresses it in eloquent terms:

> That happiness which is full of content and peace is found only in enduring ties with others, which reach to such depths that they go below the surface of conscious experience to form its undisturbed foundation. No one knows how much of the frothy excitement of life, of mania for motion, of fretful discontent, of need for artificial stimulation, is the expression of frantic search for something to fill the void caused by the loosening of the bonds which hold persons together in immediate community of experience. If there is anything in human psychology to be counted upon, it may be urged that when man is satiated with restless seeking for the remote which yields no enduring satisfaction, the human spirit will return to seek calm and order within itself. This, we repeat, can be found only in the vital, steady, and deep relationships which are present only in an immediate community [LW 2:368–69].

There is one more point to be made regarding Dewey's meaning of the social and of the good. It is that, according to him, the relationships among humans, as well as between humans and other objects in the environment, are natural and internal to the objects related. He deems it mythical to suppose that humans are born in a separate, isolated state and that some artificial device is needed to form a society. "Social ties and connections are as natural and inevitable as are physical" (LW 7:227).

In the process of distinguishing between the valued as object of sheer desire and as the valuable or reasonable good, Dewey did not wish to disregard desires or to denigrate them. In fact, one of the main purposes of the *Ethics* was to show not only that reason and desire are not opposed but that they ought to be integrated for the full development of the moral person. On the one hand, ethics should assist the individual to fulfill the objective role of judge in separating true values from the spurious. Otherwise moral judgment and conduct will be at the mercy of emotion and passion. But at the same time desires and emotions should not be excluded. The observer should be sympathetic as well as impartial. To influence behavior, the moral judgment must be enhanced by feeling (LW 7:269–70). Without this, morals can become bleak and harsh. The ideal, of course, is that our desires go out to ends which are consonant with reason. But desires should also be formed so that the one making a moral judgment may also take pleasure in it (LW 7:196). In the present context, this means that Dewey wanted the individual to appreciate the attractiveness of achieving the welfare of all so that the individual might voluntarily and joyously engage in such activity (LW 7:302–303). The primary reason, then, why individuals should be moral, should choose their true good, is that the good itself is worthy of their admiration and of their free choice.

From the above discussion it can be seen that Dewey's meaning of person, moral theory, and social philosophy are all of a piece. For him, a person is *social*, one whose very being as person consists in relationships with others for the mutual development of all. A human being is a *moral* person, since each individual assumes the responsibility of working out aims and ideals for the community and of striving for their attainment by cooperative effort. The means of achieving goals is the scientific method, which he insisted should be applied to morals. In this sense, intelligence itself is "moral" since it serves moral ends.

In his explanation of the moral good, Dewey has fulfilled one function of ethics as included in his original definition, namely, that of dealing with conduct insofar as it is good. But the definition states that ethics also deals with conduct as right or wrong, as making demands upon us, as obliging us. James Gouinlock has claimed that for Dewey theories of intelligence, value, and morals are identical, that Dewey was concerned with means–consequences and intelligent ways of bringing about welcome results and not about should, ought, right, or wrong.[14] My purpose now is to oppose that position and to recover some important aspects of Dewey's ethics, namely, those dealing with moral law, obligation, rights, and duty. Dewey begins by noting that in morality obligation and authority hold a prominent place and that they seem to be quite different from satisfaction or end, even when these latter are reasonable. The imperious character of obligation has led some to conclude that the morally good is that which is commanded and that the purpose of morals is to abide by rules, to respect authority, and to be true to the right. Now, Dewey rejects this exclusive emphasis since "mere compulsion has no moral standing" for it separates law and duty from human impulse and purpose (LW 7:214–18). Moreover, preoccupation with duty does not take into consideration the demands of concrete situations, duty becomes a fetish, and the letter of the law becomes more important than its spirit. This prevents the opening of the heart to the attractiveness of the true good. Our strongest motivation comes from a wholehearted recognition of the values and interests that bind people together (LW 7:233).

Nonetheless the presence of right and wrong cannot be ignored, and their relation to the good must be delineated. Dewey admits that the ideas of right and wrong include an element which is outside the idea of the good, namely, demand. "The Good is that which attracts; the Right is that which asserts that we ought to be drawn by some object whether we are naturally attracted to it or not" (LW 7:217). Does this mean, however, that the good and the right are distinct and separate in fact? Dewey claims that they are not, and he sets out to show that, though law, obligation, duty, and right differ in concept from that of the good, they arise out of the same relationships. He tries to establish this point by referring to the inherent natural relationships that exist between persons. Ends which make claims on conduct grow out of the social position or function of the agent and consequently out of actions which one is committed to perform by the social connections between the self and others. As examples of these relationships, Dewey cites parents, children, and friends, landlords and tenants, vendors and purchasers, trustees and beneficiaries, legislators, judges, assessors, and sheriffs.[15] One could enumerate many more. These relationships, and hence the claims and duties arising from them, are not imposed from without by external force. They are internal, even when physical or mental pressures are brought to bear to ensure their observance (LW 7:217–19). From this, Dewey draws the following conclusion:

> If we generalize such instances, we reach the conclusion that Right, law, duty, arise from the relations which human beings intimately sustain to one another, and that their authoritative force springs from the very nature of the relation that binds people together [LW 7:219].

Or again, right expresses the manner in which persons bound by intrinsic ties should be regulated in the pursuit of the benefits that all pursue in common. On the other hand, wrong consists in being unfaithful to the demands of others, since one pursues one's own advantage and neglects the common welfare (LW 7:218–19, 230–31).

It can be seen, then, that the conception of right has an independent status, though it ultimately has a close connection with that of the good. For besides the fact that they both depend on the same relationship, the role and effect of right are to lead the individual to arrive at a concept of the true good by showing that nothing is really good unless it is a benefit to others; right also shows that one *ought* to pursue the welfare of others—in other words, that the welfare of others ought to become one's true good.

> The essence of the claim which Right puts forth is that even if the thing exacted does not appeal as his good to the one to whom it is addressed, he *should* voluntarily take it to be a good; that, in short, it should *become* his good, even if he does not judge it so at the time. The element of the "should" or "ought" is what differentiates the idea of the Right from that of Good [LW 7:229].

Dewey pursues the matter from the perspective of law. He raises the question about the ultimate nature of moral authority. In order to answer the question, one must distinguish between general law and particular law. Regarding the first, he states: "Law is necessary because men are born and live in social relationships; . . . the function of law in general [is] the institution of those relations among men which conduce to the welfare and freedom of all" (LW 7:227). Again, law is "an expression of the end and good which [human] relations should serve" (LW 7:229). From these statements it can be seen that Dewey bases the meaning and need of law in general upon the internal relations that exist among human beings. This is consistent with the explanation that he gave regarding right and indeed regarding the meaning of the social as philosophic category. The social is a generalized expression of human relationships, and at the same time it states the conditions in which demands arise. At first the human being in the immature state of a child is confronted with particular relations within the narrow range of the family circle and becomes aware of specific duties. But as the child matures, there develops a general sense of obligation that is distinct from particular regulations. Dewey calls this "a new attitude toward further special situations." He compares it to a general idea, for example, of a table. This idea is a "*principle* of action" which can be used as an ideal or standard by which to judge particular existing tables or to invent new ones (LW 7:232). The general moral law fulfills a similar function regarding particular laws, as the following discussion shows.

A particular law is "a special means of realizing the function of law in general" (LW 7:227).[16] It has the authority of general law behind it, but only if the conduct that is characterized as obligatory does in fact contribute to the general welfare, that is, only if it is an instance of general law. If it does pass the test, then the individual "must, in the degree to which he is fair-minded, acknowledge it to be a common good, and hence binding upon his judgment and action" (LW 7:230). Moreover, because particular laws are specific applications of general law, they are open to examination and criticism. But if someone does challenge a given law and claim that it is unjust because it does not meet the criterion of general law, "the burden of proof is on him." He must appeal to the general law and show in what way the particular law does not meet the standard (LW 7:229–31). Dewey also speaks about a general sense of duty, right, and obligation. These are in effect the general moral law from the standpoint of the person bound by the law. "The proper function of a general sense of duty is to make us sensitive to the relations and claims involved in particular situations." Dewey adds that it is needed in time of temptation when the immediate pull of desire draws us away from the fulfillment of a particular law. On these occasions, "a generalized sense of right and obligation is a great protection" (LW 7:232).

In the light of the discussion, I would tentatively propose the following propositions as being faithful to Dewey's thought on the matter. These propositions will also serve as a summary of what has been said so far regarding moral law. (1) Law in its primary sense means general moral law. (2) Law serves as a principle, standard, ideal of what constitutes good and right conduct for human beings. (3) The primary function of law is not coercive but directive; that is, it first points out the true good, though it also imposes an obligation to seek the good. (4) The concept of law and obligation and the reciprocal notions of right and duty are distinct as concepts from that of the good, though they are related to it since all of these are founded on the same relationships. (5) Particular laws, and for Dewey these include positive laws, derive their authority from general law. (6) Legal theory is a part of ethics.

From all that has been said so far, it should be clear that law and obligation have a very important place in Dewey's ethics. For one thing, the moral ought is more than an esthetic ought. For example, it can be said that one "ought" to admire Michelangelo's *Pietà* because it is a superb work of art. But if one did not appreciate it, we would not on that account alone call the person immoral. In Dewey's terms, however, we would call parents immoral if they did not provide for their children's needs because they would violate the rightness of a relationship that obliges individuals in that relationship to behave in certain ways. The child has a claim upon the actions of the parents, while in turn parents are obliged to meet these claims. Moreover, the force of right has the effect of obliging one to do the good even if one is not attracted to it or does not judge it to be good at the time. Finally, the authority of particular laws and the real obligation arising from them are ultimately grounded in the general moral law.

Likewise it follows that in his moral philosophy Dewey was interested in more than intelligent inquiry so as to ensure the attainment of the best ends or consequences. To be sure, he was deeply concerned about this, but he went a step further. As we have seen, the only genuine ends of human endeavor are those which contribute to the welfare of all, and as humans we are obliged—really obliged—to pursue these ends. And since Dewey felt that intelligent inquiry was the best if not the only instrument in modern times to achieve these ends, he was anxious that it be available to all members of society and that it be applied to human affairs. From this we can conclude that he was aiming not only at achieving intelligent inquiry so as to bring about welcome outcomes, but also at showing the obligations consequent upon being human. Thus it can be said that intelligent inquiry and reflective morality are identical, but not in the sense that ethics collapses into logic or epistemology, thereby losing its special character. Rather, since intelligent inquiry has for its purpose the sorting out of the true moral good from its counterfeits, and the attaining of that good, it is raised to the status of the moral and shares its distinctive character.

The previous discussion has had for its purpose to develop the meaning of the good and the role of law and obligation in Dewey's ethics. There are doubtlessly many other questions that emerge from this endeavor. I shall attempt to deal with only two of these questions since they bear directly on our topic. The first is this: Granted that we can call Dewey's moral philosophy a "moral law" ethics, can we in any sense speak of it as a "*natural* moral law" ethics? The second question is really a double one: How would Dewey formulate the general moral law, and is it debatable, as is particular law?

If by natural moral law we mean the form in which it was developed in medieval scholastic philosophy, or even by Locke, then obviously the answer to the first question would have to be negative. For the medievalists held positions which Dewey would never accept. For example, natural law included a metaphysics wherein all nature is a product of God's creative act and wherein creatures are directed to their specific ends by divine providence according to an eternal law. Humans discover their own end and proper good through the natural law, which is a manifestation of the eternal law as applied to human beings and which is known by the light of natural reason. By reason one comes to know the various prescriptions of the natural law. All this, of course, would be quite alien to Dewey's ethics.

At first glance it would seem that Enlightenment theories of nature would be more acceptable to Dewey. For these did away with God entirely or at least muted his influence over the work of his creation. Moreover, nature became the book of revelation in which the solution of the mysteries of the world was to be found, and reason became the instrument of discovery. It was Hume who urged that we examine human nature for the help it could give in knowing science, natural religion, and morality. Dewey certainly agreed that the source of morality is to be sought in human nature, but he differed regarding the latter's meaning. By now it should be abundantly clear that his theory of moral law is grounded on relations and that these relations are natural to humans. In fact, relations between all objects in reality are natural. Dewey argued this point in his refutation of empiricism, idealism, and rational-ism. In his moral theory, he went on to explain the distinctive character of the social as philosophic category and the manner in which the concept of moral law is derived from the natural human relations existing within that category. This analysis is revelatory of at least some of the intrinsic forces that he claimed were at work in a common human nature. This is why Dewey also rejected theories which asserted that humans are by nature individual and that it is only by some kind of pact that they become associated in common life. In sum, then, while Dewey is in no sense a natural moral law philosopher in the classical meaning, he did base his moral theory on human nature understood in a relational way. From it he derived general principles which transcend particular obligations, whether these arise out of normal relations such as those between parents and children or out of institutionalized regulations and laws such as those in the state.

We come now to the question regarding the manner in which Dewey would formulate the general moral law. At the outset one could ask: In posing this question, are you not attempting to do something which Dewey himself consistently refused to do? This point is in need of clarification. It is certainly true that he was opposed to drawing up a catalogue of virtues and vices, rights and wrongs, do's and don'ts. He also repudiated casuistry, which he labeled as the attempt "to foresee all the different cases of action that may conceivably occur, and provide in advance the exact rule for each case." Dewey denounced all this because it allows no room for re-evaluation in the light of new facts, it tends to exag-gerate the letter of the law as opposed to its spirit, it reduces moral conduct to legalism, and most of all it drains moral conduct of freedom and spontaneity (LW 7:277–78). Consequently he thought it was more important for ethics to encourage the habit of subjecting desires to the criticism of reflective morality than to draw out in detail the instances of the good (LW 7:281).

Whatever one might say about the validity of Dewey's criticism of casuistry, it should be noted that he is not rejecting general principles but the attempt to spell out in precise and enduring terms the *specific instances*. It is difficult to believe that he was simply unconcerned about such instances. Perhaps he erred in the direction of being too wary of hard and fixed rules. Be that as it may, his complaint is against precise and timeless rules and regulations that are detached from changing situations, and not against general principles and standards. As our entire discussion has shown, Dewey has drawn up a general standard for the good and has argued for a general concept of right and duty. The standard is a "standpoint for survey of situations" in comparison with which conduct is examined and judged (LW 7:281). That standard, of course, is the common good, as he has stated it in many different ways and in a variety of contexts. To the point, then, the general moral law would seem to be best expressed in the principle: One ought to act so as to promote the common welfare and avoid what hinders it. I suppose it could be stated in other slightly different terms, but the one proposed will do.

The question as to whether or not the general moral law is debatable would seem to be easily answered. For, one could argue, it is common knowledge that as a pragmatist Dewey held that all beliefs are hypotheses subject to constant re-evaluation and possible revision in the light of new facts. It follows that no principles are unchanging or permanent. Yet we find Dewey making some rather curious statements. I have already pointed out his position on the general moral law. In addition, he states that "one cannot imagine an honest person convincing himself that a disposition of disregard for human life would have beneficial consequences" (LW 7:242). Again, at first he seems to follow the pragmatic position in alleging that, when concrete situations are considered, no fixed meaning can be given to such traditional virtues as chastity, kindness, honesty, patriotism, modesty, toleration, bravery, fair dealing, public spirit, regard for life, and faithfulness to others. Yet in the same breath he adds that in abstract form they may be permanent, since no community can endure without them (LW 7:255–56). From this and from all that Dewey has said about social arrangements and community and their relation to one's growth and development, it would seem that humans could not dispense with the general moral law or with the rather extended list of general virtues which he cites.

Hence, as vehemently as Dewey protested against a hierarchy of principles, goods, virtues, or whatever, he implicitly accepted them. They can be divided roughly into three categories: (1) the general and ultimate principle expressed in the general moral law;

(2) intermediate principles of the kind enumerated above, though the list could be extended; and (3) the particular instances of the general and intermediate principles.[17] It seems inconceivable that Dewey could ever dispense with the general or intermediate principles. To do so would render dubious, if not negate, all that he felt was required for community living, which is essential for one's development as a human being. Hence they are not debatable. The concrete instances are open to argument, not regarding the principles behind them, but only regarding their actually being genuine instances of the principles. Also, these instances can change but only according to the variety of ways in which the principles can be concretized.

The transition from Dewey's moral to his political theory is quite natural. The latter arises from his conception that a moral person develops in a community. Members of the community through intelligence project common ideals and goals which are to be achieved by cooperative effort on the part of all. It is only in union with others that persons can fully develop and mature. These ideas had been germinating early in Dewey's career and are evident in his work in education. But early too was his concern for social conditions and political events that affected or were affected by a theory of person. At Chicago he became aware of the conditions of the poor and underprivileged, and this concern remained with him all his life. On the broader level, he followed carefully the practical political decisions that were being made in national and international affairs. He became involved in public discussion and debate regarding political events, and he took sides on them—for example, the two World Wars, the League of Nations, Stalinism, and the agenda of political parties.

Dewey always contended that philosophy arises from practical problems. He exaggerates in giving the impression that this was a new concept, for many philosophers have been stimulated to develop their theories under similar conditions. But it was certainly the case that concern for concrete social issues moved him to develop his ideas. The purpose of this section is to examine his political philosophy and not to recount his involvement in political events.[18] Three of his works especially will be considered: *The Public and Its Problems* (1927), *Individualism, Old and New* (1929), and *Liberalism and Social Action* (1935).[19] Each book was written from a slightly different perspective, but they develop similar themes and there is a good deal of overlap. *The Public and Its Problems* was written to defend participatory democracy against the realist democrats who claimed that democracy should be left to the experts. But the book also deals with the origin, alterations, and weaknesses of contemporary democracy along with the causes of these weaknesses. *Individualism, Old and New* concerns itself with the origin, development, and fate of individualism in America and projects the kind of new individualism that was needed for the future. *Liberalism and Social Action* was stimulated by the rise of anti-liberalism when conservatism, liberalism, and radicalism were competing against one another. Dewey's contention was that liberalism must be rehabilitated to meet the problems of the twentieth century, and he wanted to describe the kind of radicalism that was needed to meet disturbing social conditions.[20] Consequently this book contains the longest treatment of the history of liberalism. Since the same themes recur in each book, though with different emphases, it seems best to discuss the volumes thematically rather than individually.

There are three terms which are important for Dewey's political philosophy. They are individualism, liberalism, and democracy. In terms of political theory and historical origins, Dewey uses the first two terms in almost the same sense, though individualism is more carefully nuanced when it is used to describe a theory of person as basic to liberalism. Democracy, though different from the other two, is closely related to them. Dewey's strategy is to trace historically the origin and development of individualism, liberalism, and democracy in Great Britain and their subsequent history in the United States. In *Liberalism and Social Action*, he states that the terms liberal and liberalism as identifying a particular social philosophy first appear in the early nineteenth century. But historically the movement began with Locke whom he calls "the philosopher of the 'glorious revolution' of 1688."[21] Locke maintained that, even prior to government, individuals had inherent natural rights and that government was instituted to secure these rights. This was "a rigid doctrine" that became an integral part of subsequent social theory. It also gave rise to the attitude not only that individuals and political society constituted two different centers of action but that government was the enemy of the individual. Consequently it was to the interest of the individual that government be limited as much as possible. Dewey further points out that in Locke's view property was among the natural rights of the individual. Though property had a broad meaning so as to include "life, liberty, and estates," it was property as material possessions that received the most attention from Locke and later theorists. This was to have important implications since, though Locke meant property *possessed*, the growth of commerce in Great Britain directed attention to the *production* of material goods (LW 11:6–8).

Another element that influenced the direction of liberalism in Great Britain was utilitarianism. Dewey gives a long recital of this influence, but it is sufficient to summarize its main details. Adam Smith (1723–1790) was a key figure. Concerned with social welfare, Smith felt that it could be best attained by protecting individual economic freedom and self-interest from political restraints. If many individuals improved their condition, the effect would be felt in society at large. Dewey states:

> Free economic processes thus bring about an endless spiral of an ever increasing change, and through the guidance of an 'invisible hand' (the equivalent of the doctrine of preestablished harmony so dear to the eighteenth century) the efforts of individuals for personal advancement and personal gain accrue to the benefit of society, and create a continuously closer knit interdependence of interests [LW 11:9].

Dewey notes that Locke's emphasis on property and Smith's utilitarianism served to relate natural right with private business enterprise even before the invention of the steam engine and the advent of the Industrial Revolution in England. But the new means of production in the mid-nineteenth century radically altered the situation. In the minds of liberals, those legal restrictions already in place on free commerce and exchange were looked upon with even greater hostility, and the opposition was further strengthened by the charge that social progress was being hindered. Stronger claims were therefore made for the right of individuals to use freely the new resources for wealth. Self-interest now joined hands with economic freedom to result in laissez-faire liberalism (LW 11:9–10).

Utilitarianism had its effect in another direction in the person of Jeremy Bentham (1748–1832). His goal of achieving the sum of happiness for the greatest number led him to strive for the removal of "the abuses, corruption, and inequities" of legal and political institutions. Through his writings and the activity of his disciples, Bentham affected changes in law and administration in Great Britain during the first half of the nineteenth century, and this Dewey cites as proof that liberalism could initiate radical social changes (LW 11:15). He credits Bentham too with the demise of Lockean liberalism by illustrating that consequences, not natural rights and liberties, are the chief motivating factors moving individuals to action. According to Dewey, Bentham has shown that "men do not obey laws because they think these laws are in accord with a scheme of natural rights. They obey because they believe, rightly or wrongly, that the consequences of obeying are upon the whole better than the consequences of disobeying" (LW 11:15).

So far, claims Dewey, the liberalism of the economists and that of the utilitarians were in substantial agreement. But a split between the two gradually developed. The point of contention was whether the state should be allowed to take political action for the welfare of the people. Bentham himself sided with the economists, but he allowed government intervention if it could be shown to be necessary and effective. As a matter of fact "collectivist legislative policies" increased after the mid-nineteenth century. This was due to several factors, among them the support of Tories despite their traditional opposition to the commercial class; humanitarianism fostered by religious leaders and the literary romanticists; and John Stuart Mill (1800–1873), who became increasingly aware of the value of the "inner life" and of the brutal social conditions that required some kind of social legislation (LW 11:17–19). Nonetheless, utilitarians like Bentham and Mill retained their fundamental principle that individual self-interest should be preserved. In any case, this tension led to the uncertainty in Dewey's time regarding what liberalism stood for and was a chief cause of its ineffectiveness. On the one hand were the old liberals who saw liberalism as an opposition between individual freedom and organized social action. While allowing government intervention in critical cases, "they are the confirmed enemies of social legislation." But, on the other, the majority of the liberals felt that government should do more than guarantee the rights of one individual against another. Government should take positive measures to ensure that the mass of individuals are protected from inequities. Unfortunately, however, many of these liberals who favored government intervention were still influenced by past liberal conceptions. They were satisfied with *ad hoc* measures that alleviated crisis situations but did not attempt to change radically the way individuals live and act in association (LW 11:21–22).

Before we move on to Dewey's description of the rise of liberalism and individualism in America, one more term should be examined briefly, and that is democracy, including its relation to liberalism. In *The Public and Its Problems*, Dewey maintains that there is no one best form of government as realized in the state.[22] It depends on the circumstances existing at any time. He sets down one principle, however: "the state is the organization of the public effected through officials for the protection of the interests shared by its members." Government is not the state, for the latter includes the public; "the public, however, is organized in and through those officers who act in behalf of its interests." The effectiveness of government is to be judged by its consequences and for this reason it should always be subject to evaluation. Its processes can never become so independent that they resist criticism and alteration (LW 2:252–56). Political democracy itself arose historically from a number of concrete conditions, primarily the invention of the machine and the development of industrial technology. In accord with his position regarding the development of liberalism, Dewey sees democracy as a "revolt" against existing forms of government that stifled the freedom of individual commercial enterprise and that attempted to limit these forms as much as possible. As such, then, democracy was not due to "the doctrines of doctrinaires" theoretically conceived and planned so as to follow a logical series of steps. Such characteristics as "universal suffrage, frequent elections, majority rule, congressional and cabinet government" evolved to serve a purpose, "that of meeting existing needs which had become too intense to ignore" (LW 2:144–45, 326).

In *Individualism, Old and New*, Dewey turned his attention to America. More than any other country, it had felt the effect of industrialization and the money culture resulting from it. In one respect, America seemed to have moved in a direction opposite to mainstream individualism. It had become corporate and inter-dependent, whether one considers large business mergers, accu-mulation and control of wealth, mass production and distribution of goods, contacts among people through communication and travel, or organized control of news media, entertainment, and athletics. These conditions seemed ideal for the growth of the individual. Unfortunately our corporateness is dominated by pecuniary gain, and politics is covertly used to preserve the freedom of the individual in order to control the flow of business without government interference (LW 5:58–61). The result is the "lost individual" or, better, the mass of individuals who play no part in planning and carrying out the economic enterprise. They are "hands" only and are at the mercy of those who direct eco-nomic affairs for their own financial profit (LW 5:104). Dewey admits that some government control has been exercised to miti-gate these harsh realities. But it constituted no more than Band-Aids when public outcry became too insistent to be ignored (LW 5:96–97). Consequently liberalism in America is confused; the tragedy lies in the fact that it lacks a clearly defined social philoso-phy and political theory and does not seem to know where to look to find them. It is no wonder that many claim that individualism is finished (LW 5:80).

Dewey developed in great detail the kind of liberalism that he thought was necessary if it is to be effective in the light of existing conditions. Though he described several characteristics of the new liberalism, three in particular will be mentioned. They are the meaning of the individual, a proper understanding of political democracy, and the role of science. Something has already been said about Dewey's notion of the person when his moral theory was discussed. In the present context, he states that, under the influence of Locke's philosophy and psychology, early liberalism looked upon the individual as ready-made and fully constituted prior to its association with others. All that it needed for its development was the removal of external restrictions. This set up the opposition, accepted in modern times, between the individual and the social and stimulated the search for ways to heal that breach. It was the source of the theory of natural rights possessed before society was formed and the antagonism between the individual and government that has already been described. In Dewey's view, individuals, persons, are such only to the extent that they share common ends and exercise their initiative with others in procuring those ends. The isolated individual, fully mature and capable of developing further without social contacts, is simply a myth.[23]

From this it is clear that there is no opposition between individual and community, provided, of course, that community is properly understood. His classic definition, already quoted, states that community is "conjoint activity whose consequences are appreciated as good by all singular persons who take part in it, and where the realization of the good is such as to effect an energetic desire and effort to sustain it in being just because it is a good shared by all." The essential elements of a community are unity of purpose that all share and cooperative effort to attain that purpose. It is in this context that he calls community a democracy even before he discusses its political meaning. It is a mode of association that leads to the development of a person in the fullest and richest sense. The community aims at achieving a rich quality of life that is esthetically fulfilling and that rises above material goods. It allows freedom to the individuals to use their intelligence and initiative in projecting these goals. It enables them to feel the joy of being actively engaged in the pursuit of goals and not idle spectators on the sidelines whose destiny is determined for them. This ideal was already fixed in Dewey's mind when in his work in education he had used such terms as community, society, and democracy. Democracy, then, is first of all a way of life.

It is not surprising that Dewey utilized such ideals when he spoke of political democracy. He admitted that democracy as a form of government is difficult to define, as is aristocracy or any other political system. Nonetheless he claimed that the basic issue cannot be avoided. Democracy must counter the influence of a machine age that threatens to overcome the aspirations for a higher life. In one sense he is saying that the ideals of any political system are only as high as the citizens who constitute the state. In a cynical sense, I suppose he means that you get only what you pay for. If the citizens themselves have no appreciation for the qualitative aspect of life, it can hardly be reflected in their activities. That is why he was concerned with ideals and personal cultivation which he developed so beautifully and eloquently in *Art as Experience* (1935), written about the same time as his political works. In addition, however, the question facing American democracy was whether it could arrange social conditions so that a material, industrial civilization would be successful in "liberating the mind and refining the emotions of all who take part in it." To Dewey it was evident that this was a most serious question that must be faced not only by America but by the world (LW 5:100–101).

Though Dewey was highly critical of the course that liberalism and democracy had taken in America, he was reluctant to give specific recommendations as to the precise form that political democracy should take (LW 5:89–90, 146). But he kept returning to the "lost individual" and the need to alleviate the conditions that led to the stifling of the person. So he contended that the question of how much control should be exerted by government for social ends would be the central issue in future political struggles and it must be faced by political parties (LW 5:91–96). He had little confidence that either existing major party could sufficiently detach itself from an interest in financial gain and bring about radical reforms that would make social legislation a matter of conscious policy rather than expediency. An alternative was socialism, but he felt that the term itself conjured up the myth that it necessarily meant the use of political power to distribute wealth equally among all citizens, "a kind of arithmetically fractionized individualism," or the oppressive and destructive model of Soviet Russia (LW 5:90–98). Dewey was convinced that socialism of some kind was inevitable, but for him it came down to a choice between "capitalistic or public socialism," a phrase that became the title of Chapter VI of *Individualism, Old and New*. By capitalistic socialism he meant a form that retains the status quo, in the sense that it makes some token attempts at social legislation but leaves big business free to continue its monopolies. It was this kind of socialism that he rejected. It is interesting to note that he persisted in this position even during the Roosevelt years of the 1930s, since he maintained that the president retained the policy of unplanned social change and left the economic system in the hands of the captains of industry.[24]

Dewey opted for "public socialism" or planned and ordered social development (LW 5:98). He finally settled on the term social democracy. His friends were not always completely satisfied with the term, and Dewey himself was somewhat uncomfortable with it.[25] But he thought that it was the best way to preserve liberalism as a vehicle of radical change while avoiding the extremes usually associated with socialism. He called for the socialization of the forces of production, including "the nationalization of banking, public utilities, national resources, transportation, and communication."[26] At the same time he did not believe that government control was the final answer. The new liberalism must be "the spontaneous function of communal life" (LW 5:81). He advocated, naïvely it would seem, that all citizens should be imbued with a sense of "social awareness" so that all segments of society, the captains of industry as well as representatives of labor, would join hands in developing a liberal program independent of direct government action. In *Liberalism and Social Action,* he argued that this was the lesson taught by early nineteenth-century liberalism. There is first needed informed political intelligence without which direct action may very well end in political irresponsibility (LW 11:14).

The last aspect of Dewey's social and political theory to be treated here is science. In large measure it contrasts sharply with Peirce's use of science in moral and social matters. Neither Peirce nor Dewey restricted science to laboratory procedures, though Peirce was more fully conversant with the physical sciences. As we have seen, the latter did have something to say about the social aspect of science, but it was rather confined. Dewey's social and political theory is extensive, and science as standing for the experimental method of hypothesis, test, and evaluation of consequences is integral to every phase of his philosophy. So it should not be surprising that it enters into his political theory and that he manifests his bias against fixed norms and principles. This is evident in his criticism of Locke's theory of natural law and rights and in his historical approach to political systems in which consequences are the ultimate test of their validity. One of the requirements of liberalism and democracy, whether these be considered as a theory of person or as a political system, is freedom of inquiry. Though the experimental method has been applied to the physical sciences, people are still reluctant to use it in human concerns, more especially social institutions. In a strong statement, he attributes many social ills to this failure: the slave-like conditions of men, women, and children; slum conditions; poverty; exploitation of nature; and the destructive forces of war. In other terms, science is controlling the person, whereas the opposite should be the case.

In this context, Dewey makes some revealing remarks about his attitude toward science. He seems to be taking a stand in favor of "applied" over "pure" science. Familiar is his position that all thinking and inquiry begin with concrete problems. This in itself may be open to debate, but he pushes it further when he discusses pure science. In relation to social ills that demand attention, he indicts the "glorification" of pure science as an escape, a haven of refuge, an avoidance of responsibility. Pure science in its genuine sense does not exclude utility. Again in strong terms he maintains that "the adulteration of knowledge is due not to its use, but to vested bias and prejudices, to one-sidedness of outlook, to vanity, to conceit of possession and authority, to contempt or disregard of human concern in its use." Science is knowledge worthy of honor only when it is applied to human affairs. In this sense it is "humanistic" and not limited to special industrial use for private gain. He labels it a "caricature" to suppose that inquiry and reflection entail the desertion of libraries, laboratories, and research for the sake of social reform. More research, not less, is needed as long as it does not become preoccupied with knowledge without reference to human problems.[27] In addition, the science that he espouses is not the work of single individuals; it is a public, community affair, accessible to all both in the procedures of conducting it and in the accessibility of its results. It can be seen, then, that community and democracy include freedom of inquiry carried out by cooperative effort for the good of all.

The criticism that Dewey levels against pure science in the context of social reform is quite severe. In his behalf, it should be remembered that he was deeply disturbed by the plight of the underprivileged and by the misuse of technology in industrial matters. It could be argued, therefore, that he is not criticizing science as such but technology. In other places his treatment of pure and applied science is more balanced and detached.[28] But even there he expresses his conviction that science should see its fulfillment in the application to concrete problems.

NOTES

1. For a more detailed treatment of Peirce's ethics, see Potter, *Charles S. Peirce: On Norms and Ideals*, esp. pp. 31–42.

2. Letter of Peirce to James, December 26, 1897, in Ralph Barton Perry, *The Thought and Character of William James*, 2 vols. (Boston: Little, Brown, 1935), II, 419.

3. For my own development of Peirce's "Neglected Argument," see my article "Is Peirce's Pragmatism Anti-Jamesian?" *International Philosophical Quarterly*, 5 (1965), 541–63.

4. Colapietro, *Peirce's Approach to the Self*, pp. 69–75. See also CP 5.229–36.

5. Colapietro, *Peirce's Approach to the Self*, p. 73.

6. Peirce's criticism of James has been developed by Colapietro. See ibid., pp. 37–38, 62–63, 78, 101.

7. The essay "The Moral Philosopher and the Moral Life" is found in *The Will to Believe and Other Essays in Popular Philosophy*, pp. 141–62. References to the essay are included in the text as WB with page reference.

8. I do not think it is too wide of the mark to suggest that this norm is very similar to Hume's "standard of taste."

9. I have developed this in "The Religious Philosophy of William James," *Thought*, 41 (1966), 249–81.

10. See James's letters in Frederick J. Down Scott, ed., *William James: Selected Unpublished Correspondence, 1885–1910* (Columbus: Ohio State University Press, 1986), pp. 121, 206, 355, 361, 364–65.

11. Dewey's insistence on relations and connections as against the classical empiricists can be found in a number of places—for example, "The Need for a Recovery of Philosophy," MW 10:12, 24; "The Inclusive Philosophic Idea," LW 3:41–45.

12. See *Art as Experience*, Chapter 1, "The Live Creature," LW 10:9ff., and *Logic: The Theory of Inquiry*, Chapter 2, "The Existential Matrix of Inquiry: Biological," LW 12:30ff.

13. "The Inclusive Philosophic Idea," LW 3:43–44.

14. James Gouinlock, *John Dewey's Philosophy of Value* (New York: Humanities, 1972), pp. 3, 310–12.

15. Dewey's list includes a wide variety of human associations and the obligations arising from them. Those between parents and children appear to be more "ordinary" or "natural" than those between landlords

and tenants. But Dewey viewed them all as manifestations of the internal relationships between people. It would seem, though, that he should have made some further refinements.

16. In accordance with the preceding note, it would seem that by particular laws Dewey means particular instances arising from various kinds of human associations, of which some are more natural and others are formally instituted by positive legislation. Again, further distinctions on Dewey's part would have helped.

17. Again, particular instances include particular obligations arising from ordinary relations and from those instituted by government.

18. For detailed accounts of Dewey's involvement in politics, see Robert B. Westbrook, *John Dewey and American Democracy* (Ithaca: Cornell University Press, 1991), and Gary Bullert, *The Politics of John Dewey* (New York: Prometheus, 1983).

19. Sidney Hook called *Liberalism and Social Action* "a masterly analysis of the social and political philosophy of liberalism" and "a book which may very well be to the twentieth century what Marx and Engels' Communist Manifesto was to the nineteenth." *John Dewey: An Intellectual Portrait* (New York: John Day, 1939), p. 158. Westbrook states that *The Public and Its Problems* was Dewey's only work of formal political philosophy. See his *John Dewey and American Democracy*, p. 300. I suppose one could argue about what constitutes political philosophy and how it differs from social philosophy. Dewey himself uses both terms, sometimes interchangeably and sometimes together. In my view, the three works under discussion should be classed as his formal development of a social and political philosophy.

20. See Dykhuizen, *Life and Mind of John Dewey*, p. 265.

21. It is well known that Peter Laslett has mounted a strong refutation of the theory that Locke wrote the *Second Treatise* to justify the "Glorious Revolution." See his edited volume of Locke's *Two Treatises of Government*, Introduction, pp. 45–66.

22. In spite of this "no best form of government" position, it soon becomes quite clear that Dewey's theory of the social dimension of the person would require some form of democracy in government.

23. Dewey makes these points in several places, for example, *Individualism, Old and New*, LW 5:121–22; *The Public and Its Problems*, LW 2:290; *Liberalism and Social Action*, LW 11:30.

24. See Westbrook, *John Dewey and American Democracy*, p. 440, Bullert, *Politics of John Dewey*, p. 149.

25. Westbrook, *John Dewey and American Democracy*, pp. 429–30.

26. Ibid., p. 441.

27. *The Public and Its Problems*, LW 2:344–45; *Individualism, Old and New*, LW 5:107–8.

28. For example, see *Experience and Nature*, LW 1:128–31; *Knowing and the Known*, LW 16:25–56.

6

NEW DIRECTIONS AND NEGLECTED CHALLENGES

IN THE PREFACE, it was said that the task of this volume was to indicate the new directions taken by American pragmatism away from the stream that, to a great extent at least, had set it on its course. At this point, it might be helpful to detach oneself from the varied and complex details that were involved and take a broader view of these two traditions. In the course of the previous discussion, some observations, favorable and unfavorable, were offered. Now it might be opportune to bring together some of the leading ideas and to evaluate them for whatever help they may give in meeting contemporary problems.

In general, both empiricists and pragmatists were united in their rejection of classical metaphysical theories of substance and *a priori* reasoning. Emphasis was placed on sense data as central to philosophical reflection. From this perspective, the pragmatists were well within the empirical tradition. But to use James's phrase, the pragmatists insisted that empiricism should be "radical."

Whatever else this term meant, it indicated that connections were more important than disjunctions, both in experience and in reality. This had a profound effect in epistemology, for it put the knower and the known in direct relationship. Peirce set the stage for this approach by accepting the reality of things recurring in our experience. These he called "indubitables," not that they were beyond doubt, but that we do not in fact doubt them unless something occurs in our experience that prompts us to do so. In that case we initiate the process of inquiry and re-examine the hypothesis, test it, and reconfirm or change it. Inquiry, then, begins in doubt. This reduces considerably the "epistemological problem" of the empiricists regarding how one moves from idea to reality. It is not a naïve realism but the application of test and consequences, "controlled inquiry," resulting in warranted assertions. It eliminates Hume's torturous attempts to bridge the gap with imagination, feignings, and fictions. It also breaks away from Hume's rigid definition of certainty and allows for both the rejection of absolute certitude in matters of fact and a reasonable account of what one takes to be knowledge. The distinction between the philosophic and the ordinary view is removed. Peirce's fallibilism and common-sensism also confronted the rigid determinism of the late nineteenth century. He was able to draw upon his theory of abduction and induction about which Hume knew very little. One anomaly among the pragmatists is Dewey's treatment of cause and effect. As we saw in Chapter 2, he somewhat inconsistently restricted it to human purposes or ends-in-view. In this he seems to have overreacted against cause since, in his view, it was closely associated with metaphysical notions, such as "occult powers," fixed essences, and final causes. Nonetheless, the pragmatists' approach to knowledge about matters of fact seems in the main reasonable and in accord with contemporary scientific thinking.

It is in the social dimension of the person that relations have their most fruitful effects. Once the break was made from empirical atomism, the door was open to see the importance of relations in human association. This begins with Peirce and is gradually extended, reaching its culmination in Dewey's social and political theory. In Chapter 4 I have suggested that another reading of Hume brings to light his awareness of the sentiments and feelings that human beings have for one another. In this regard, I think that commentators in general, and Dewey in particular, have interpreted Hume's theory of person too atomistically and have neglected its relational aspects. On Dewey's behalf, it should be said that, when he criticizes the reduction of the person to an isolated individual, he generally attributes that position to the "empirical tradition" or to "classical empiricism." In *Reconstruction in Philosophy*, he states that "the individualistic school of England and France in the eighteenth and nineteenth centuries was empirical in intent" (MW 12:190). He mentions Locke by name in his account of the history of liberalism and individualism, and it is Locke who bears the brunt of his criticism. But I would suspect that Dewey included Hume in his indictment of empiricism regarding the person. For all that, he is correct in attributing the atomism of the individual to the influence of the British empiricists, Locke directly and Hume at least by his overall approach to reality. And even in his attribution of sympathy as a component of human nature, Hume does not propose a social philosophy approaching that of the pragmatists. In fact, in his political theory, common opinion and consensus become blurred and offer little on which to build a theory of community.

As we have seen, for Dewey democracy is first of all a community, a social mode of association, and only then a political system. He consistently refused to discuss the precise details for implementing his recommendations for political democracy. Some may look upon this as a legitimate stance for a political philosopher as distinct from a political scientist. In actuality his hesitancy was one of the main reasons why in the end his form of liberalism and democracy never reached maturity or acceptance. There can be little doubt that his proposals often seem naïve and highly idealistic. He was not adept in the rough-and-tumble world of politics, and he had no idea how to exert political pressure to see that ideas took root.

Yet we live in an age of cynicism regarding America's democratic system of government. The reasons are many and complex, and I suppose there is little agreement as to what those reasons are or how they should be addressed. But perhaps it is time to consider anew the ideals that should be the underpinning for humanity in general and for any particular organization of government. Philosophers seem to specialize in projecting aims and purposes that may never be completely fulfilled. In *Republic* V, when Socrates proposed his philosopher-king, a ruler who had a love of wisdom, truth, and justice, he made the prediction that without this, there was no hope for humanity. One may disagree with one-person rule or with Socrates' meaning of the philosopher. But without ideas, without a renewal of vision, without mutual trust and a willingness to engage in sharing common goals and purposes, any form of government will fail. I believe that Dewey was convinced of this. It is the reason why he tirelessly advocated democracy and why he never wavered in his faith and confidence in it.

Though there is a rich social dimension to the pragmatists' meaning of self, there is also paradoxically a surprising shallowness. They had a bias against the metaphysical notion of substance, they were wary of any tendency toward atomism in a theory of person, and they harbored an empiricist fear of subjectivism. Consequently experience and the self seems constituted by what goes on between the individual and some other person or thing. Relation, transaction, and interdependence thereby become objectified, and this perspective can seem to lean toward behaviorism. As fruitful as the social dimension of the self can be for community and human associations, there is need at times for self-reflection, self-understanding, self-evaluation, assumption of personal responsibility, soul-shaking choices that deeply affect the self, regret, sorrow, and resolution to alter one's way of life. Though perhaps these internal affairs are often, if not always, outer-related, they are not essentially social acts but ones that only the individual can make. No one else can decide, act, or assume responsibility in another's stead. This aspect of the self seems even more needed today than it was when the pragmatists were living. Dewey warns that the individual can become a prey to "the frothy excitement of life, of mania for motion, of fretful discontent, of need for artificial stimulation." There are elements in our present culture which tend to move the individual in precisely that direction. Someone has called the present the "stereophonic age" (it could also be called "audiovisual"), for people seem to have a constant need of exposure to sight and sounds without which they are empty and lost. Dewey recognized this tendency, though I suspect he would be appalled at the extent to which it has developed. It is a manifestation in a more radical way of a reluctance to seek the quietude of inner reflection and meditation that is necessary for the mature growth of the person. I do not think that the pragmatists' notion of the self was in their day or is now deep enough or rich enough to respond to the inner needs of the self.

Another matter for re-examination is the place of feelings and emotions in moral judgment. This has long been a source of debate, and opinions have ranged from a dismissal of them to their wholesale acceptance as a basis for moral distinctions. Hume can be ranked among the latter since he made moral judgment to consist solely in approval or disapproval based on sentiment. Moral good and evil are found, not in actions or objects, but in the affections of a human nature that is common to all of us. This is consistent with the purpose that he assigns to moral theory, namely, to teach us our duty by manifesting the beauty of virtue and the ugliness of vice, and to move us to form habits by which we embrace the one and avoid the other. On a positive note, some credit should be given to Hume for bringing forward the affective side of the person. Moral judgments rarely involve cold, calculated decisions but are made in the context of deep emotional stress. Whatever role a moralist may assign to the affections, they cannot be ignored. Hume, of course, was not alone in highlighting feelings. One need only recall Anthony Ashley Cooper (1671–1713), the third Earl of Shaftesbury; Francis Hutcheson (1694–1747), whose writings more directly influenced Hume; and Adam Smith (1723–1790). All of these postulated some "moral sense" akin to sentiment or to esthetic discernment regarding beauty and ugliness, and they emphasized feelings and sentiments as the sole determinant in moral judgment.

In an essay "Of the Standard of Taste," Hume makes an attempt to base morality on the same standard of taste that humans use in assessing beauty. It is the thesis that he had proposed in the *Treatise*. What he is seeking is "a *Standard of Taste*, a rule by which the various sentiments of men may be reconciled; at least a decision afforded confirming one sentiment, and condemning another" (E 234). Hume is convinced that "all the general rules of art [and of morals too] are founded only on experience, and on the observation of the common sentiments of human nature" (E 237). He admits that there will be disagreements among individuals on this point. Certain conditions are needed for correct judgments, for example, a healthy state of our senses, both external and internal, exposure to beautiful art objects, and freedom from prejudice. Against the objection that even then there may be some disagreement, Hume responds that this is true even regarding "theories of abstract philosophy, systems of profound theology," which by the way have been exploded, to be succeeded by other systems and theories (E 248). This seems to be a weak reply, as though his own position were no better or worse than any other. But he immediately returns to his strong endorsement of the esthetic sense by giving examples which, he maintains, exhibits a unanimity of judgment regarding taste. Anyone claiming that, regarding genius and eloquence, Ogilby is superior to Milton, or Bunyan to Addison, would be thought to be as mistaken as one who asserts that a pond is as extensive as the ocean (E 235). He further presumes it to be universally agreed that "Aristotle, and Plato, and Epicurus, and Descartes, may successively yield to each other: but Terence and Virgil maintain an universal, undisputed empire over the minds of men. The abstract philosophy of Cicero has lost its credit: the vehemence of his oratory is still the object of our admiration" (E 249). These examples may well reveal Hume's own preference in literature, but they hardly sustain his argument regarding a universal agreement in matters of beauty and morals.

The pragmatists resisted the move to the exclusive acceptance of any moral or esthetic sense. But in varying degrees they tried to incorporate feelings into their moral theory. Peirce was the most cautious of all three pragmatists. His overall purpose was to answer the one question that must be answered before the answers to all other questions could be given. That question had to do with a vision of the ultimate purpose and destiny of the universe, a vision that he called esthetic, in his own meaning of the term. Once this was appreciated, it could direct feelings and sentiments in individual situations. James was sensitive to human responses regarding the beautiful and the ugly and to the attractive and repulsive qualities of various actions. He recognized that these influence judgment in moral matters though he also maintained that such judgments were never absolute. At the same time he rejected a skeptical point of view, and so the moralist must seek the "most organizable good" that is consistent with a more conclusive whole. Dewey perhaps more than the others tried to integrate desires and duty into an ethical theory. He criticized the exclusive emphasis on duty and obligation, and he highlighted the role of sympathy, whereby we put ourselves in another's place and try to see things from the other's perspective. This leads to an expanded personality. In *Ethics* he states that "through sympathy the cold calculation of utilitarianism and the formal law of Kant are transported into vital and moving realities" (LW 7:271). Nonetheless Dewey insists on the dominant role of reason and of a sense of duty which together control desires and lead to the formation of desires in accord with reason. In all, it would seem that, whatever else one may wish to say about their moral theories, the pragmatists were more successful than Hume in balancing reason and desire, duty and sentiment.

One issue that often surfaces in discussions of moral theory is the place of obligation. Perhaps it would be well to start with a description of what it means. Vincent Cooke expresses it as follows: "By moral obligation I mean the fact that there are certain things that I ought to do whether I want to do them or not. For instance, I ought to be just, to speak the truth, and keep my promises, whether I have a particular desire to do so or not."[1] Of course, what I ought to do and what I feel like doing often coincide, but it is the former that constitutes the essential element of obligation. With this as a background, let us focus on what our five philosophers have said about moral obligation and its foundation.

Locke has recourse primarily to natural law. It is an expression of those rights that he claimed to be inherent in human nature and ultimately given by God. Natural law includes a divine imperative to act according to the law, with rewards or punishments imposed for conformity with or violations of the law. Natural law is also the basis for civil law, as he tried to argue in the *Second Treatise*. In effect, one has the obligation to respect the rights of others because ultimately these rights and the duties implied in them are God-given. Citizens should obey the laws of the realm because they have for their purpose the protection of natural human rights. But he neither did nor could justify his position through his empiricist philosophy. In *An Essay Concerning Human Understanding*, Locke claimed that, in practical life, a third law, the law of opinion and reputation, is the most persuasive. People abide by rules and customs approved by society because they fear the condemnation and disgrace resulting from actions that go against the general opinion of those with whom they associate.

But in both the *Essay* and the *Second Treatise*, natural law is the foundation of natural rights and obligations in both the state of nature and civil society.

Hume has little to say explicitly about moral obligation. He was more interested in redefining the meaning and origin of judgments regarding virtue and vice. The ultimate grounding of such judgments is human nature which we all share, and the feeling of sympathy for others which under proper conditions will overcome the tendency to self-interest. Nonetheless, Bernard Wand has argued that Hume, despite denials by some critics, does give an account of obligation.[2] Wand shows that, though Hume held for a natural sympathy for others, accounting for judgments regarding virtue and vice, he did not leave room for a natural tendency to moral obligation. The latter is generated by several factors. One is habit whereby a person acts in certain ways because of their attractiveness and feels compelled to continue in those modes of behavior (T 522, 551). Another is the "artifice of politicians" who exhort their subjects to esteem the practice of justice in order that they may govern more easily and that the peace of society may be maintained (T 500, 523). Hume adds, however, that the urging of politicians would be worthless unless there is in nature a sentiment for justice. Education that children receive from parents also reinforces the natural esteem for justice (T 500). Wand maintains, then, that in Hume's opinion moral obligation arises not from a natural sentiment but from social forces. Concern for public interest is not a sufficient stimulus to moral actions, but "we regard ourselves as being obliged to act justly only because, according Hume, we have in the past been sufficiently instructed, disciplined and habituated."[3] I think that Wand has given a careful and faithful rendition of Hume's position on moral obligation.

Peirce did not treat ethics in the "usual" sense, so it is not surprising that he did not address the question of moral obligation. Ethics for Peirce was placed in the context of his evolutionary ontology and teleology, and so he was interested in the reason beyond all reasons, the answer to the question beyond all questions. This was to serve as a general guide for how human beings should act in particular circumstances if they were to act reasonably. His aim was to point out what it means to achieve the full potential of a human person who by nature is endowed with the intelligence to know "our scheme of the universe" and to understand "the fitness of what conduct ought to be." In doing this, Peirce professed to be going against "the subtle and ineradicable narrowness of most modern philosophy" which was to reduce ethics to judgments of beauty and taste, thereby making them purely subjective. At the same time, he did not neglect the esthetic attractiveness of his ideal, for it presented that which is admirable in itself and deserves our positive response. Moreover, in his development of the social self, he tried to open our minds to the satisfaction and fulfillment that can be attained when one cooperates with others in bringing individuals and the universe itself to their final completion. In the last analysis, then, why *ought* we to be moral? Because that is the only way in which we can fulfill ourselves as persons; otherwise we would turn away from that which is both attractive and reasonable.

There remains the question regarding the role of God in Peirce's moral theory. As Donna Orange shows, for Peirce God is the expression of Reason in nature, yet beyond anything that now exists. Reasonableness entails an intelligent author of nature, creating and energizing it, and *God* is the ideal term of evolution.[4] And yet, Peirce does not envision God as a supreme legislator ordering obedience to commands. He emphasizes the "God is love" of St. John's Gospel. It is "the formula of an evolutionary philosophy, which teaches that growth comes only from love," a love that inspires us to assist other persons in fulfilling their aspirations and to breathe life into the evolutionary process, even its hateful elements, making it lovely. Peirce laments the fact that in the Book of Revelation St. John slips back into condemnation and punishment and seems to forget the message of universal love (CP 6.287, 289, 311). It seems that in his early life Peirce was disturbed by the "angry squabbles" between the Calvinists and the Unitarians and the "mere denials" on which they concentrated.[5] His approach to God and religion thereafter emphasized the attractiveness of love rather than the repugnance of fear and punishment.

James in his moral theory was trying to cope with several notions: a middle ground between absolutism and relativism, obligation, and God. In his essay, "The Moral Philosopher and the Moral Life," obligation was considered in relation to what he called the metaphysical question. He states that, if there be a God, then the deity is the model and source of obligation. This was proposed in opposition to those who would hold that there is no objective criterion for moral judgment. Yet the criterion is not absolute, since God is finite. But James does not advance much beyond that. Though God is prominent throughout the rest of the essay and in the final chapter of *Pragmatism*, the emphasis is on the invitation that God extends to human beings to cooperate with one another for their own fulfillment as persons rather than on a divine imperative. He set all this in the context of a "richer universe" and "the most organizable good." This aspect of James's thought has some similarities with Peirce's metaphysical scheme, though in James it is only lightly suggested.

Dewey does introduce law, duty, and obligation into his moral theory. Though he makes it clear that for him compulsion alone has no moral standing, he is just as clear in his position that we *ought* to seek the good, namely, cooperative effort for the welfare of the community—and this even though one is not naturally attracted to it or does not judge it to be good at the time. The obligation arises from the relationships existing among human beings and the special character of those relationships which we ought to, has the duty to, recognize.

If one considers obligation to be an essential element in moral theory, there are strengths and weaknesses in the positions advanced by both empiricists and pragmatists. Locke proposes a traditional form of the natural law theory which includes goods, rights, duties, and a supreme lawgiver who imposes an obligation with rewards or punishments appropriate to one's response to the law. But he did not substantiate his theory philosophically. Hume strongly emphasizes common opinion or consensus, but he uses the term loosely and does not sharply define what consensus means or indicate how common or widespread it should be. In the last analysis, Hume seems to derive obligation from existing social norms, and in this respect it appears to be a slightly different version of Locke's law of opinion or reputation. Peirce presents a powerful metaphysical scheme which could be accommodated to classical natural law, though he says little about obligation. James is ambivalent, defending obligation as an antidote to relativism but not incorporating it into his final position. Dewey wants obligation to be an essential aspect of his moral theory, but it is not clear why one ought to act morally even when at the time one is not attracted to it.

As Cooke has pointed out, the key to the problem of moral obligation consists in how strong a sense it is to be taken. He claims that many ethicians have either abandoned a belief in God or do not perceive that such a belief provides sufficient grounds for moral obligation. They therefore settle for a milder "ought" which prompts us to act in ways that will further "human flourishing," something which everyone presumably desires. Variations on this theme can be found even among Neo-Aristotelians and Neo-Thomists who propose loyalty to humanity, or choosing principles behind a veil of ignorance, or organization of life according to human well-being.[6] Cooke claims that these principles do not answer the problem of one who says: "I know that it is reasonable that I do such and such (e.g., avoid an act of treachery, adultery, or sodomy), but I do not want to do it." Cooke asks a question of his own and attempts an answer.

> In what sense can he be said to be obliged to do what, in accord with the canons of practical reasoning, he should do, if he does not want to do it? Assuming that the only ends are ends which by particular choices I myself set either *ad hoc* or as part of some larger life plan, then I am always able to reverse these choices and reject the ends. An account of moral obligation in terms of the rational necessity of means to ends requires an ultimate end that is prior to any particular act of the will and that is thus necessarily willed. If by a particular act of the will I determine that I do not want to do such and such and if doing such and such is something that I necessarily will as a constitutive part of or means to my ultimate end, then indeed I can be convicted of internal contradiction or irrationality. But this solution, which I think is correct, is only open to those who argue for a necessary object of human willing, and the only plausible account of such a necessity at the foundation of our willing is a metaphysics of human nature.[7]

Cooke goes on to claim that there is a distinction between a pursuit of goods set by nature and one regarding particular goods freely and arbitrarily chosen. The former requires a metaphysics that includes the creative activity of God as its ultimate explanation.

I would certainly endorse the main lines of Cooke's position. It is too large a question to go into now, but I do believe that a viable theory of moral obligation can be sustained only according to this model or something like it. Elsewhere I have argued for an obligation in terms of an "absolutely imperative but noncompulsory necessity."[8] By this I mean that, while leaving the person free, a moral obligation to be truly meaningful must be one that is not left to the individual's choice to be obliged or not. The individual cannot choose not to be obliged. An example would be the case of one who is overpowered and robbed. The victim would say that the attacker *ought not* to have done that, even though the attack was not witnessed by a third party and cannot be proved in a court of law. An ethician might reason that the attacker is obliged to live according to his or her nature as a human being and so should not commit a violent attack against another. But then the attacker could respond: "I don't feel like living that way. And if I am frustrating my development as a person, call me stupid, not immoral." I find it difficult to believe that the victim would be satisfied with such an answer. In effect, this response indicates that the attacker has reduced morality merely to rationality, and one could ask why a person is *obliged* to act rationally and what is the force of the obligation. It seems to me that, if obligation is to be truly binding, as a victim would insist, it must be unconditional, that is, not subject to one's choosing to be obliged or not. And if that is the case, obligation requires a lawgiver who is superior to human beings, able to make demands upon them and to impose appropriate sanctions.

Finally I would express regret that Locke's attempt to bring natural law into moral and political discourse ended in failure and gradually to its eventual demise.[9] As Cooke has shown, there have been attempts to retrieve natural law theory and give it a respectable place in contemporary moral discussion. It may be too soon to predict how far such a move will go, for there are critics outside the tradition and differences of opinion within it. But natural law deserves another look so that it may be presented in its authentic form and not in truncated versions.

Surely there are other "new directions" and "neglected arguments" that could be selected and discussed. But these are the ones that have occurred to one observer of the empiricist and pragmatic traditions. If they are found to be inadequate, I would paraphrase Hume's concluding remarks to his attempts to propose a coherent theory of person. "For my part, I confess that further insights are too hard for my understanding. I pretend not to pronounce my observations as complete. Others, perhaps, more mature than I, may discover things that have surpassed my comprehension" (T 636).

NOTES

1. Vincent M. Cooke, S.J., "Moral Obligation and Metaphysics," *Thought*, 66 (1991), 65.

2. Bernard Wand, "Hume's Account of Obligation," *Philosophical Quarterly*, 6 (1956), 155–68.

3. Ibid., 163.

4. Donna Orange, *Peirce's Conception of God: A Developmental Study* (Lubbock: Texas Tech University, 1984), pp. 68–69, 77.

5. C. S. Peirce to Smith, July 25, 1908, Scientific Correspondence, cited in Murray G. Murphey, *The Development of Peirce's Philosophy* (Cambridge, Mass.: Harvard University Press, 1961), p. 15.

6. Cooke, "Moral Obligation and Metaphysics," 68.

7. Ibid., 69–70.

8. See my articles "Moral Obligation and God," *The New Scholasticism* 54 (1980), 265–78, and "Moral Obligation—With or Without God?" ibid., 59 (1985), 471–74. In note 4 of his article, Cook notes what he takes to be a difference between his position and mine. Actually our positions are closer that he indicates.

9. For the gradual decline of the laws of nature as enunciated in the Declaration of Independence, see Carl L. Becker, *The Declaration of Independence* (New York: Vintage, 1944), pp. 233ff. For the influence of natural law in America, see Andrew J. Reck, "Natural Law in American Revolutionary Thought," *The Review of Metaphysics*, 30 (1977), 686–714.

BIBLIOGRAPHY

The bibliographical material for any one of the philosophers treated in this volume is, of course, enormous. I have selected those books and articles which especially influenced my own thinking. But in the main I have concentrated on the works of philosophers themselves, with particular attention to those which bear more directly on the themes of the chapters.

PRIMARY SOURCES

Locke, John. *An Essay Concerning Human Understanding.* Ed. Peter N. Nidditch. Oxford: Clarendon, 1984.
———. *Two Treatises of Government.* Ed. Peter Laslett. London: Cambridge University Press, 1988.
Hume, David. *Dialogues Concerning Natural Religion.* Ed. Norman Kemp Smith. New York: Bobbs-Merrill, 1947.
———. *Enquiries Concerning Human Understanding and Concerning the Principles of Morals.* Ed. L. A. Selby-Bigge. 3rd ed. rev., P. H. Nidditch. Oxford: Clarendon, 1979.
———. Essays Moral, Political and Literary. Oxford: Oxford University Press, 1974.
———. The History of England from the Invasion of Julius Caesar to the Revolution of 1688. Ed. W. B. Todd. 6 vols. Indianapolis: Liberty Classics, 1983.
———. A Treatise of Human Nature. Ed. L. A. Selby-Bigge. 2nd ed. rev., P. H. Nidditch. Oxford: Clarendon, 1980
Peirce, Charles Sanders. Collected Papers of Charles Sanders Peirce. Edd. Charles Hartshorne, Paul Weiss, Arthur W. Burks. 8 vols. Cambridge: Belknap Press of Harvard University Press, 1933–1958.
James, William. *Essays in Radical Empiricism.* Cambridge: Harvard University Press, 1976.
———. *A Pluralistic Universe.* Cambridge: Harvard University Press, 1977.
———. *Pragmatism and the Meaning of Truth.* Cambridge: Harvard University Press, 1981.

————. *The Principles of Psychology*. 3 vols. Cambridge: Harvard University Press, 1981.

————. *The Will to Believe and Other Essays in Popular Philosophy*. Cambridge: Harvard University Press, 1979.

Dewey, John. *The Early Works of John Dewey, 1882–1898*. 5 vols. Carbondale: Southern Illinois University Press, 1967–1972.

————. *The Middle Works of John Dewey, 1899–1924*. 15 vols. Carbondale: Southern Illinois University Press, 1976–1983.

————. *The Later Works of John Dewey, 1925–1953*. 17 vols. Carbondale: Southern Illinois University Press, 1981–1991.

SECONDARY SOURCES

Aaron, Richard I. *John Locke*. 3rd ed. Oxford: Clarendon, 1971.

Allen, Gay Wilson. *William James: A Biography*. New York: Viking, 1967.

Ashcroft, Richard. *Revolutionary Politics and Locke's Two Treatises of Government*. Princeton, N.J.: Princeton University Press, 1986.

Becker, Carl L. *The Declaration of Independence*. New York: Vintage, 1944.

Bernstein, Richard J. *John Dewey*. New York: Washington Square, 1967.

————. *Praxis and Action: Contemporary Philosophies of Human Activity*. Philadelphia: University of Pennsylvania Press, 1971.

Boring, Edwin G. *A History of Experimental Psychology*. New York: Appleton-Century-Crofts, 1950.

Buchler, Justus, ed. *Philosophical Writings of Peirce*. New York: Dover, 1955.

Bullert, Gary. *The Politics of John Dewey*. New York: Prometheus, 1983.

Capaldi, Nicholas. *David Hume, The Newtonian Philosopher*. Boston: Twayne, 1975.

Colapietro, Vincent Michael. *Peirce's Approach to the Self: A Semiotic Perspective on Human Subjectivity*. New York: State University of New York Press, 1989.

Collins, James. *A History of Modern European Philosophy*. Milwaukee: Bruce, 1954.

Cooke, Vincent M., S.J. "Moral Obligation and Metaphysics." *Thought*, 66 (1991), 65–74.

Copleston, Frederick, S.J. *A History of Philosophy*. Vol. V. Westminster, Md.: Newman, 1964.

Cranston, Maurice. *John Locke*. New York: Arno, 1979.

Danford, John W. *David Hume and the Problem of Reason*. New Haven: Yale University Press, 1990.

Descartes, René. *The Philosophical Works of Descartes*. Trans. Elizabeth S. Haldane and G. R. T. Ross. 2 vols. New York: Dover, 1955.

Dooley, Patrick Kiaran. *Pragmatism as Humanism: The Philosophy of William James*. Chicago: Nelson-Hall, 1974.

Dunn, John. *The Political Thought of John Locke*. Cambridge: Cambridge University Press, 1969.

Dykhuizen, George. *The Life and Mind of John Dewey*. Carbondale: Southern Illinois University Press, 1973.

Fontinell, Eugene. *Self, God, and Immortality: A Jamesian Investigation*. Philadelphia: Temple University Press, 1986.

Gallie, W. B. *Peirce and Pragmatism*. Harmondsworth: Penguin, 1952.

Goudge, Thomas A. *The Thought of C. S. Peirce*. New York: Dover, 1969.

Gouinlock, James. *John Dewey's Philosophy of Value*. New York: Humanities, 1972.

Grasso, Kenneth L. "The Emergence of the Liberal Doctrine of Toleration in the Thought of John Locke." Ph.D. diss., Fordham University, 1988.

Harré, R., and Madden, E. H. *Causal Powers: A Theory of Natural Necessity*. Oxford: Blackwell, 1975.

Hendel, Charles W. *Studies in the Philosophy of David Hume*. Rev. ed. New York: Bobbs-Merrill, 1963.

Hook, Sidney. *John Dewey: An Intellectual Portrait*. New York: John Day, 1939.

Jessop, T. E. "Some Misunderstandings of Hume." In *Hume: A Collection of Critical Essays*. Ed. V. C. Chappell. Garden City, N.Y.: Doubleday, 1966. Pp. 35–52.

Kemp Smith, Norman. *The Philosophy of David Hume*. New York: St. Martin's, 1964.

Knight, Thomas S. *Charles Peirce*. New York: Washington Square, 1965.

Langford, Paul. "The Eighteenth Century (1688–1789)." In *The Oxford History of Britain*. Ed. Kenneth O. Morgan. New York: Oxford University Press, 1988. Pp. 399–469.

Leyden, W. von, ed. *John Locke: Essays on the Law of Nature*. Oxford: Clarendon, 1954.

Livingston, Donald W. *Hume's Philosophy of Common Sense*. Chicago: The University of Chicago Press, 1984.

Livingston, Donald W., and King, James T., eds. *Hume: A Re-Evaluation*. New York: Fordham University Press, 1976.

Miller, David. *Philosophy and Ideology in Hume's Political Thought*. Oxford: Clarendon, 1981.

Moore, Edward G., and Robin, Richard S., eds. *Studies in the Philosophy of Charles Sanders Peirce*. Second Series. Amherst: University of Massachusetts Press, 1964.

Mossner, Ernest Campbell. *The Life of David Hume*. Oxford: Clarendon, 1980.

Murphey, Murray G. *The Development of Peirce's Philosophy*. Cambridge: Harvard University Press, 1961.

Noxon, James. *Hume's Philosophical Development*. Oxford: Clarendon, 1973.

O'Connell, Robert J., S.J. *William James on the Courage to Believe*. New York: Fordham University Press, 1984.

Orange, Donna. *Peirce's Conception of God: A Developmental Study*. Lubbock: Texas Tech University, 1984.

Perry, Ralph Barton. *The Thought and Character of William James*. 2 vols. Boston: Little, Brown, 1935.

Phillipson, Nicholas. *Hume*. New York: St. Martin's, 1989.

Potter, Vincent G., S.J. *Charles S. Peirce: On Norms and Ideals*. Amherst: University of Massachusetts Press, 1969.

Reck, Andrew J. *Introduction to William James*. Bloomington: Indiana University Press, 1967.

————. "Natural Law in American Revolutionary Thought." *The Review of Metaphysics*, 30 (1977), 686–714.

Reilly, Frances E., S.J. *Charles Peirce's Theory of Scientific Method*. New York: Fordham University Press, 1970.

Richardson, R. C. *The Debate on the English Revolution Revisited*. 2nd ed. New York: Routledge, 1988.

Rockefeller, Steven C. *John Dewey: Religious Faith and Democratic Humanism*. New York: Columbia University Press, 1991.

Roth, John K. *Freedom and the Moral Life*. Philadelphia: Westminster, 1969.

Roth, Robert J., S.J. *American Religious Philosophy*. New York: Harcourt, Brace, 1967.

————. "David Hume on Religion in England." *Thought*, 66 (1991), 51–64.

————. "Is Peirce's Pragmatism Anti-Jamesian?" *International Philosophical Quarterly*, 5 (1965), 541–63.

————. *John Dewey and Self-Realization*. Englewood Cliffs, N.J.: Prentice-Hall, 1962.

————. "Locke on Ideas and the Intuition of the Self." *International Philosophical Quarterly*, 28 (1988), 163–69.

————. "Moral Obligation and God." *The New Scholasticism*, 54 (1980), 265–78.

————. "Moral Obligation—With or Without God?" *The New Scholasticism*, 59 (1985), 471-74.

————. "The Religious Philosophy of William James." *Thought*, 41 (1966), 249–81.

Scott, Frederick J. Down, ed. *William James: Selected Unpublished Correspondence, 1885–1910*. Columbus: Ohio State University Press, 1986.

Sleeper, R. W. *The Necessity of Pragmatism: John Dewey's Conception of Philosophy*. New Haven: Yale University Press, 1986.

Smith, John. *Purpose and Thought: The Meaning of Pragmatism*. New Haven: Yale University Press, 1978.

———. *The Spirit of American Philosophy*. Rev. ed. Albany: State University of New York Press, 1983.

Stewart, John B. *The Moral and Political Philosophy of David Hume*. New York: Columbia University Press, 1963.

Stroud, Barry. *Hume*. Boston: Routledge & Kegan Paul, 1977.

Thompson, Manley. "Peirce's Experimental Proof of Scholastic Realism." In *Studies in the Philosophy of Charles Sanders Peirce*. Second Series. Edd. Edward C. Moore and Richard S. Robin. Amherst: University of Massachusetts Press, 1964. Pp. 414–29.

———. *The Pragmatic Philosophy of C. S. Peirce*. Chicago: The University of Chicago Press, 1953.

Wand, Bernard. "Hume's Account of Obligation." *Philosophical Quarterly*, 6 (1956), 155–68.

Westbrook, Robert B. *John Dewey and American Democracy*. Ithaca: Cornell University Press, 1991.

Wexler, Victor G. *David Hume and the History of England*. Philadelphia: The American Philosophical Society, 1979.

Wild, John. *The Radical Empiricism of William James*. New York: Doubleday, 1969.

Wood, Neal. *The Politics of Locke's Philosophy*. Berkeley: University of California Press, 1983.

Woozley, A. D., "Introduction." *John Locke: An Essay Concerning Human Understanding*. New York: New American Library, 1974.

Wright, John P. *The Sceptical Realism of David Hume*. Minneapolis: University of Minnesota Press, 1983.

Yolton, John W. *John Locke and the Way of Ideas*. Oxford: Oxford University Press, 1956.

———. *Locke: An Introduction*. New York: Blackwell, 1985.

———. *Locke and the Compass of Human Understanding*. Cambridge: Cambridge University Press, 1970.

INDEX

Aaron, Richard I., 27*n*4, 133*n*11
Adaptation, in Dewey, 24, 26, 84
Allegiance to government, in Hume, 117–18, 120–22, 125–26
Aquinas, Thomas, 50
Aristotle, 4, 6, 50, 77–78, 80–82, 84, 105, 138, 187
Atomism, 2, 185; in Dewey, 87, 158, 183–84; in Hume, 8–11, 27, 34, 37, 58, 75, 77, 119, 148, 183; in James, 16, 48, 147; in Locke, 5–7, 11, 32, 77, 99; in Peirce, 11, 77, 183

Bacon, Francis, 23
Bain, Alexander, 149
Becker, Carl L., 194*n*9
Behaviorism, 1, 15, 185
Belief, and realism, 44; in Dewey, 26, 50–52, 56, 157, 168; in Hume, 10, 36, 40, 108, 111; in James, 21, 47, 150, 152–56, 192; in Locke, 3, 23; in Peirce, 12–14, 44, 58, 146, 156
Bentham, Jeremy, 149, 172
Boring, Edwin G., 89*n*6
Boyle, Robert, 5, 31, 58, 82, 105
Buchler, Justus, 11, 28*n*10
Bullert, Gary, 180*nn*18 & 24

Cause and effect, in Dewey, 49–57; in Hume, 10, 33–37; in James, 44–49; in Locke, 29–33; in Peirce, 37–44
Charles I, 99, 126–28, 135
Charles II, 128
Civil theology, in England, 100
Civil War, in England, 99, 102, 107, 123, 128, 135*n*25
Colapietro, Vincent M., 78–79, 89*n*3, 144, 179*nn*4–6
Collins, James, 100, 133*n*7
Common consent, *see* Consensus
Common-sensism, in Peirce, 12, 183
Comte, August, 50
Concrete reasonableness, in Peirce, 140–41, 156
Connections, in Dewey, 52–57, 157–62, 179; *see also* Continuity

Consciousness, 1; in Hume, 71; in James, 15–17; in Locke, 60–65
Consensus, in Hume, 125–32
Consent theory, in Hume, 120–22; in Locke, 101
Continuity, 2; in Dewey, 22–27, 54–55; in Hume, 10; in James, 15–22, 71–72; in Peirce, 11–14
Cooke, Vincent M., s.j., 188, 192–94, 194*nn*1, 6–8
Cooper, Anthony Ashley, 99, 186
Copleston, Frederick, s.j., 2, 27*n*2
Cranston, Maurice, 27*n*4, 133*n*11, 134*n*13
Custom, and belief in Hume, 10, 36–40

Democracy, in Dewey, 170–79
Democritus, 50
Descartes, René, 1–4, 11–13, 50, 60, 82, 95, 105, 187
Desires, in Dewey's moral theory, 160–61
Dewey, John, adaptation, 24; and Aristotle, 50, 80–81; *Art as Experience*, 22, 24–25, 55, 176; belief, 26, 50–52, 56, 157, 168, and realism, 44; cause and effect, necessary connection, 49–57, connections, 52–57, 157–58, 160, 162, 179, and community, 159–161; continuity, in experience, 22–27, between knower and known, 26–27, in cause and effect, 52–55; democracy, 170–79, and liberalism, 170–77, and community, 175, 184, and science, 177–79; *Democracy and Education*, 22; desires, 161; "Development of American Pragmatism," 84; duty, *see* Obligation; emotions, 160, 187; empiricism, classical, 23, 25, 27, 55, 87, 158, 184; ends, 54–57; *Essays in Experimental Logic*, 22, 49; esthetics, 25, 160–61; *Ethics*, 156–57, 160–68, 188; experience, 22–27; *Experience and Education*, 22; *Experience and Nature*, 22–24, 49, 56, 85, 87–88, 181*n*28; feelings, 161;